JUSTICE SOCIETY of AMERICA

THY KINGDOM COME PART ONE

DAN DIDIO SENIOR VP-EXECUTIVE EDITOR **MICHAEL SIGLAIN** EDITOR-ORIGINAL SERIES **HARVEY RICHARDS** ASSISTANT EDITOR-ORIGINAL SERIES
ANTON KAWASAKI EDITOR-COLLECTED EDITION **ROBBIN BROSTERMAN** SENIOR ART DIRECTOR **PAUL LEVITZ** PRESIDENT & PUBLISHER
GEORG BREWER VP-DESIGN & DC DIRECT CREATIVE **RICHARD BRUNING** SENIOR VP-CREATIVE DIRECTOR **PATRICK CALDON** EXECUTIVE VP-FINANCE & OPERATIONS
CHRIS CARAMALIS VP-FINANCE **JOHN CUNNINGHAM** VP-MARKETING **TERRI CUNNINGHAM** VP-MANAGING EDITOR **ALISON GILL** VP-MANUFACTURING
DAVID HYDE VP-PUBLICITY **HANK KANALZ** VP-GENERAL MANAGER, WILDSTORM **JIM LEE** EDITORIAL DIRECTOR-WILDSTORM **PAULA LOWITT** SENIOR VP-BUSINESS & LEGAL AFFAIRS
MARYELLEN MCLAUGHLIN VP-ADVERTISING & CUSTOM PUBLISHING **JOHN NEE** SENIOR VP-BUSINESS DEVELOPMENT **GREGORY NOVECK** SENIOR VP-CREATIVE AFFAIRS
SUE POHJA VP-BOOK TRADE SALES **STEVE ROTTERDAM** SENIOR VP-SALES & MARKETING **CHERYL RUBIN** SENIOR VP-BRAND MANAGEMENT
JEFF TROJAN VP-BUSINESS DEVELOPMENT, DC DIRECT **BOB WAYNE** VP-SALES

Cover by Alex Ross

JUSTICE SOCIETY OF AMERICA: THY KINGDOM COME PART ONE

DC Comics, 1700 Broadway, New York, NY 10019 | A Warner Bros. Entertainment Company | Printed in Canada. First Printing. HC ISBN: 978-1-4012-1690-0 SC ISBN: 978-1-4012-1741-9

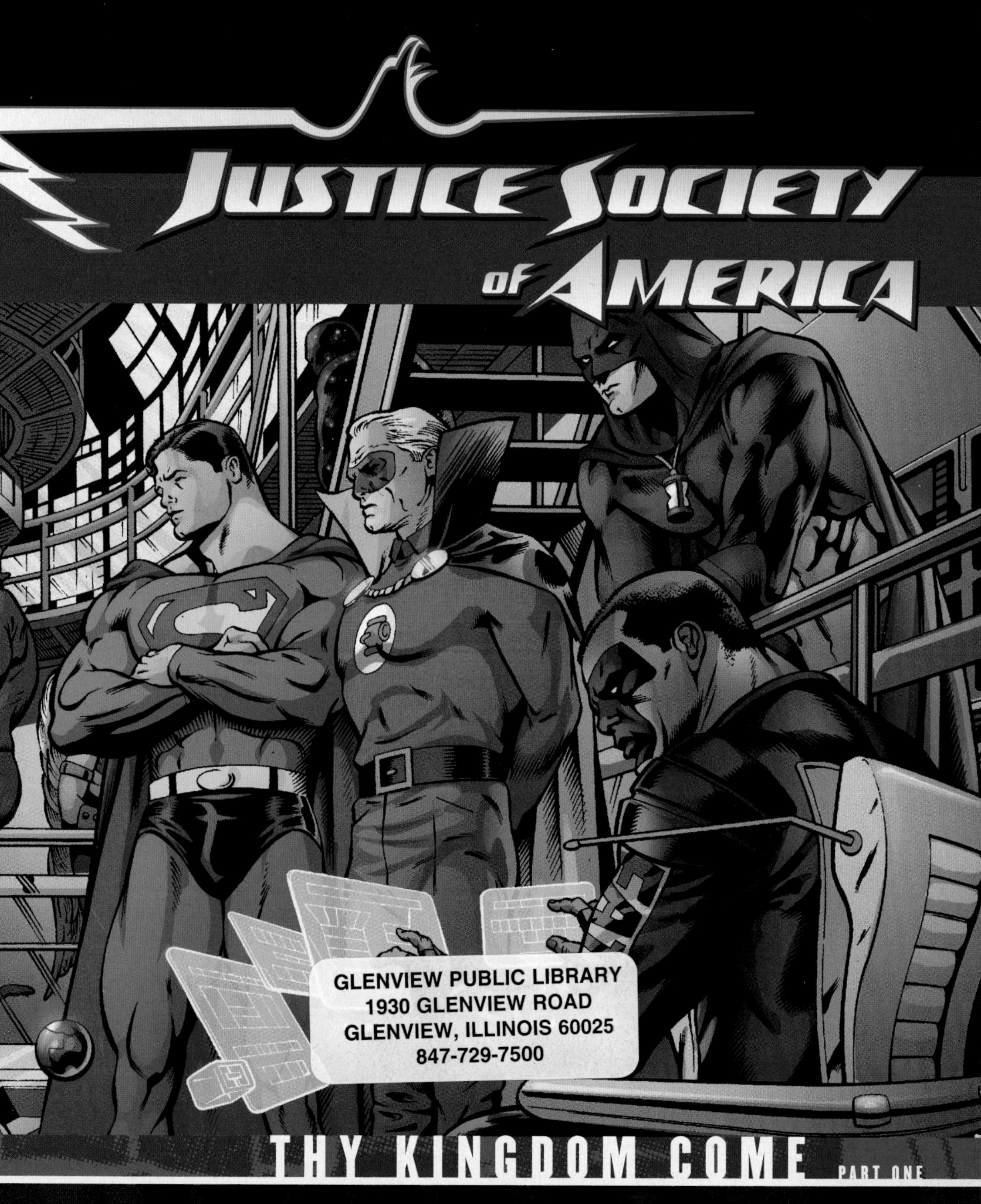

THY KINGDOM COME PART ONE

"THY KINGDOM COME" STORY BY **GEOFF JOHNS & ALEX ROSS** WRITER **GEOFF JOHNS**

PENCILLERS **DALE EAGLESHAM FERNANDO PASARIN**

PAINTED KINGDOM COME SEQUENCES BY **ALEX ROSS**

INKERS **RUY JOSÉ RODNEY RAMOS DREW GERACI**

COLORISTS **JEROMY COX ALEX SINCLAIR JOHN KALISZ HI-FI**

GREEN LANTERN Engineer Alan Scott found a lantern carved from a meteorite known as the Starheart. Fulfilling the lamp's prophecy to grant astonishing power, Scott tapped into the emerald energy and fought injustice as the Green Lantern. His ring can generate a variety of effects and energy constructs, sustained purely by his will.

THE FLASH The first in a long line of super-speedsters, Jay Garrick is capable of running at velocities near the speed of light. A scientist, Garrick has also served as mentor to other speedsters, and to many heroes over several generations.

WILDCAT A former heavyweight boxing champ, Ted Grant, a.k.a. Wildcat, prowls the mean streets defending the helpless. One of the world's foremost hand-to-hand combatants, he has trained many of today's best fighters — including Black Canary, Catwoman, and the Batman himself.

HAWKMAN Originally Prince Khufu of ancient Egypt, the hero who would become known as Hawkman discovered an alien spacecraft from the planet Thanagar, powered by a mysterious antigravity element called Nth metal. The unearthly energies of the metal transformed his soul, and he and his love Princess Chay-Ara were reincarnated over and over for centuries. Currently he is Carter Hall, archaeologist and adventurer.

POWER GIRL Once confused about her origins, Karen Starr now knows she is the cousin of an alternate-Earth Superman — who gave his life in the Infinite Crisis. Her enhanced strength and powers of flight and invulnerability are matched only by her self-confidence in action, which sometimes borders on arrogance.

MR. TERRIFIC Haunted by the death of his wife, Olympic gold medal-winning decathlete Michael Holt was ready to take his own life. Instead, inspired by the Spectre's story of the original Mr. Terrific, he rededicated himself to ensuring fair play among the street youth using his wealth and technical skills to become the living embodiment of those ideals. He now divides his time between the JSA and the government agency known as Checkmate.

HOURMAN Rick Tyler struggled for a while before accepting his role as the son of the original Hourman. It hasn't been an easy road — he's endured addiction to the Miraclo drug that increases his strength and endurance, and nearly died from a strange disease. Now, after mastering the drug, he uses a special hourglass that enables him to see one hour into the future.

LIBERTY BELLE Jesse Chambers is the daughter of the Golden Age Johnny Quick and Liberty Belle. Originally adopting her father's speed formula, Jesse became the super-hero known as Jesse Quick. After a brief period without powers, Jesse has returned — now taking over her mother's role. As the new Liberty Belle, Jesse is an

DR. MID-NITE A medical prodigy, Pieter Anton Cross refused to work within the limits of the system. Treating people on his own, he came into contact with a dangerous drug that altered his body chemistry, enabling him to see light in the infrared spectrum. Although he lost his normal sight in a murder attempt disguised as a car accident, his uncanny night vision allows him to protect the weak under the assumed identity of Dr. Mid-Nite.

SANDMAN Sandy Hawkins was the ward of the original Sandman Wesley Dodds, and he is the nephew of Dodds's lifelong partner, Dian Belmont. After a bizarre accident, Hawkins was able to transform himself into a pure silicon or sand-form. Recently, he has been experiencing prophetic dreams. He also carries a gas mask, gas guns and other equipment.

STARGIRL When Courtney Whitmore discovered the cosmic converter belt that had been worn by the JSA's original Star-Spangled Kid (her stepfather, Pat Dugan, was the Kid's sidekick Stripesy), she saw it as an opportunity to cut class and kick some butt. Now called Stargirl, she divides her time between her adventures with the JSA and bickering/teaming up with Pat — who sometimes monitors Courtney from his S.T.R.I.P.E. robot.

DAMAGE Grant Emerson has had a difficult life. Growing up, he was the victim of an abusive foster father. Then later, after discovering his explosive powers, he accidentally blew up half of downtown Atlanta. Last year, he was almost beaten to death by the super-speed villain known as Zoom. Grant has worn a full-face mask as Damage ever since.

STARMAN A mysterious new Starman recently appeared in Opal City, saving its citizens numerous times. He apparently suffers from some form of schizophrenia, and hears voices in his head. Voluntarily residing in the Sunshine Sanitarium, Starman will occasionally leave and use his gravity-altering powers to fight crime.

WILDCAT II Tommy Bronson is the newly discovered son of original Wildcat Ted Grant. But it's not quite "like father, like son" here. For one thing, Tom doesn't want to be a fighter like his dad. And second, this new Wildcat has the ability to turn into a feral creature, with enhanced agility and animalistic senses...

CITIZEN STEEL The grandson of the original Steel, Nathan Heywood is a former football hero who has suffered numerous tragedies. First, an injury and infection required his leg to be amputated. Then, a vicious attack by the Fourth Reich wiped out most of his family. But during the attack, a bizarre incident left him with metal-like skin and superhuman strength.

CYCLONE Maxine Hunkel is the granddaughter of the original Red Tornado, Abigail

PREVIOUSLY...

Determined to rebuild the Justice Society of America, founding members Green Lantern, Flash and Wildcat initiate an unprecedented recruitment program, tracking the bloodlines of heroes across the world to bring in new members. Previous JSA members Hawkman, Power Girl, Mr. Terrific, Sandman, Dr. Mid-Nite, and a new Starman (who is seemingly from the future) join the ranks as well as younger heroes Stargirl, Hourman, Liberty Belle, Damage and Cyclone.

But just as the Society welcomes the rookie heroes, the immortal villain Vandal Savage, with the help of the Fourth Reich, initiates his plans to assassinate the original members of the JSA, and all of their descendants. During a surprise attack at a Heywood family reunion (relatives of Hank Heywood, the original Commander Steel), most of the family is killed — leaving only a few children left alive, as well as Hank's grandson, Nathaniel, who is accidentally exposed to a strange liquid metal during the onslaught.

Elsewhere, original Wildcat Ted Grant discovers he has a grown-up son, Tommy Bronson — who can turn into a "were-panther" creature. While Tommy has no desire to become a fighter, or follow in his father's footsteps, a confrontation with Vandal Savage proves that Tommy — with the help of his superhuman agility — can still hold his own. After the JSA defeats Savage, Ted inducts Tommy as the newest member of the JSA.

Shortly afterward, the Justice Society teams up with the Justice League, as they discover that several members of the Legion of Super-Heroes from the 31st century (where new member Starman claims to come from) are in the present. The JLA and JSA eventually track down all seven Legionnaires, seeking to discover why these heroes of the future have traveled back in time. When the mystery is soon solved, most of the Legion members decide to go back to the future, but Starman elects to stay in the present.

JUSTICE SOCIETY OF AMERICA #7 cover A by ALEX ROSS

JUSTICE SOCIETY OF AMERICA #7 cover B by DALE EAGLESHAM & RUY JOSÉ Interior art by EAGLESHAM, JOSÉ & RODNEY RAMOS ROD REIS

THEY CALLED MY GRANDFATHER COMMANDER STEEL.
HE'S BEEN DEAD FOR YEARS, BUT I CAN STILL SEE HIM SITTING UP ON THAT PICNIC TABLE. TELLING US HIS STORIES.
LIKE HOW HE WAS MORE NERVOUS ABOUT ASKING MY GRANDMOTHER TO MARRY HIM THAN LANDING AT NORMANDY.
HEYWO
THE DAY THEY LIBERATED PARIS, HE SHRUGGED OFF THREE BOMBSHELLS AND A MORTAR ATTACK. THAT NIGHT HE SAID LOVE FILLED THE CITY STREETS.
HE SENT MY GRANDMOTHER A TELEGRAM THE NEXT DAY. "WILL YA?" SHE SENT HIM A TELEGRAM BACK. "SURE."
MY GRANDFATHER TOLD US, "NEVER COMMIT TO ANYTHING YOU WOULDN'T DO FOREVER." THEY WERE MARRIED OVER SIXTY YEARS.
I WOULD'VE PLAYED BALL EVEN LONGER IF I COULD'VE.
AND NOT JUST FOR ME. IF I'D GONE PRO, I WOULD'VE PUT MY BROTHER AND MY COUSINS THROUGH COLLEGE. MOM COULD'VE STOPPED WORKING TWO JOBS.
MY FAMILY'S FUTURE WAS SUPPOSED TO BE IN SAFE HANDS.
BUT I BECAME USELESS WHEN I TOOK THAT HIT.
MY LEG WAS AMPUTATED BECAUSE OF A MISDIAGNOSIS AND AN INFECTION I COVERED UP WITH PAINKILLERS.
THOSE PILLS... THEY'RE THE ONLY THINGS THAT GET ME THROUGH THE DAY.
THEY MAKE ME NUMB.
I WANT TO BE NUMB.
DON'T HURT THEM.

I NEED TO BE...
GET AWAY FROM MY FAMILY!
RRANKKK
RRAANKK
INDESTRUCTIBLE

GUTENMORGEN, NATHAN.
CAPTAIN NAZI.
BASHHH
MONSTER!
NATHAN! STOP!
CAPTAIN NAZI ISN'T HERE!
YOU'RE IN THE MEDICAL WING OF THE JUSTICE SOCIETY'S HEADQUARTERS! YOU'RE SAFE!
MY NAME IS DOCTOR MID-NITE.
...DOCTOR? ST-STAY BACK.
FROM THE INCISION I SAW ON YOUR LEG, I'D GUESS YOU DON'T TRUST DOCTORS MUCH. AND I CAN'T SAY I BLAME YOU.
KRAKKK
WHY AM I--?
YOU WERE IN A COMA. YOU'VE BEEN UNDER MY CARE FOR THE LAST THREE WEEKS.
WHY AM I...?
WHAT?
WHY AM I STANDING?

...STABBED REICHSMARK IN THE ONLY PLACE HE WAS VULNERABLE. THE INSIDE OF HIS THROAT.
THE MOLTEN METAL FLOWING THROUGH HIS VEINS WAS ABSORBED INTO YOUR SKIN--THE EXACT REASON WHY I HAVEN'T YET DETERMINED.
YOU WENT INTO ANAPHYLACTIC SHOCK, BUT BY THE NEXT MORNING YOUR BODY SEEMED TO STABILIZE.
THE DAY AFTER, WHERE YOUR LEG HAD BEEN AMPUTATED--
--YOU BEGAN GROWING A SOLID STEEL PATELLA, TIBIA...AN ENTIRE NEW LEG. THEN CAME THE METAL MUSCLE FIBERS.
AND NOW YOUR SKIN HAS BEEN TRANSMUTED INTO SOME KIND OF ORGANIC STEEL.
AS NEAR AS I CAN TELL, IT WOULD TAKE NOTHING LESS THAN AN AIM-9 SIDEWINDER TO EVEN KNOCK YOU DOWN.
SO PLEASE, UNTIL WE GET THAT STRENGTH OF YOURS UNDER CONTROL, DON'T TOUCH ANYTHING ELSE.
I SHOULD'VE DIED.
BUT YOU DIDN'T. YOUR PROGNOSIS IS VERY GOOD CONSIDERING EVERYTHING YOU'VE BEEN--
THEY'RE DEAD.
MY WHOLE FAMILY IS DEAD.
NATHAN... I'M SORRY.
I THOUGHT YOU KNEW...

...YOU WEREN'T THE ONLY SURVIVOR.

ST. ANTHONY'S HOSPITAL.

DESPITE THE ODDS, YOU AND HAWKMAN HURT THE FOURTH REICH.
ENOUGH THAT THEY WERE ANXIOUS TO LEAVE WITHOUT CHECKING TO SEE IF THE WOUNDED WERE DEAD. OR IF ANYONE WAS *HIDING*.
THE OLDEST ONE IN THERE, AN ELEVEN-YEAR-OLD GIRL, SHE PULLED TWO OTHERS INTO THE BUSHES.
THAT'S NICOLE. SHE'S MY COUSIN.
SHE'S THE ONLY ONE WH SPEAKING TO THE DOCTOR NURSES. NOTHING MUCH M THAN FOOD REQUEST

I WANT TO TALK TO THEM.

KRRRATCHH

NATHAN--!
I'M SORRY, I...
YOUR NERVES ARE LINED WITH THE SAME ORGANIC SHELL YOUR SKIN IS. YOU WON'T FEEL TEMPERATURE CHANGE OR BE ABLE TO TELL WHEN YOU'RE TOUCHING WOOD OR METAL OR FLESH.
I WON'T FEEL ANYTHING? FOR HOW LONG? HOW LONG AM I GOING TO BE LIKE THIS?

I CAN'T TOUCH THEM THEN, CAN I? I'D BREAK THEIR BONES.
AFTER EVERYTHING THEY'VE BEEN THROUGH I CAN'T EVEN GET **CLOSE** TO THEM.
THE JUSTICE SOCIETY MAY BE ABLE TO **FIX** THAT.

WEDNESDAY
THURSD
OPAL CITY.
...TO MAKE ME FRET, I FLY A-ROUND! I HAD STRINGS, BUT NOW I'M FREE--
SHINE
TARIUM
PAL CITY
CHIATRIC
HOSPITAL
--THERE ARE NO STRINGS ON ME! Heh heh.
GOOD AFTERNOON, STARMAN. YOU DID A VERY GOOD THING THIS MORNING, PULLING THAT SCHOOL BUS FROM THE RIVER.
WELL, TODAY SHOULD BE A GOOD DAY FOR EVERYONE, DOCTOR.
YOU SAVED A LOT OF KIDS AND MADE A LOT OF PARENTS HAPPY.
20
21
IT'S WEDNESDAY, AFTER ALL.
27
29
30
HI, STARMAN.
HI, FLOYD.
OH, YES!
THEY DON'T HAVE THESE WHEN I COME FROM.
EXCUSE ME, STARMAN.

I KNOW THE JUSTICE SOCIETY WANTS A FEW WORDS WITH YOU, BUT SINCE WE'RE OLD FRIENDS--
--I ASKED FOR SOME TIME FIRST.
I WANT TO KNOW MORE ABOUT WHAT'S HAPPENED TO THE LEGION. AND I WANT TO KNOW MORE ABOUT *YOU.*
MILK
CHOMPF
YOU 'ANNA 'OPPY 'OE, KAL?
I'D LOVE ONE, THOM.

HOW ARE YOU DOING IN THERE, NATE?
I'M FINE, MR. TERRIFIC.
PSSSHHHH
THEN HERE WE GO.
T-SPHERES. OPEN THE LINES.
VEET
YOU'RE CERTAIN THIS WILL WORK, MID-NITE?
NATE NEEDS SOMETHING TO RESTRICT HIS MOVEMENTS, CARTER. KEVLAR, EVEN CHAIN MAIL MESH, WON'T COME CLOSE TO DOING THAT.
SO MICHAEL AND I CAME UP WITH SOMETHING ELSE.
"AN EXTRA LAYER OF 'SKIN' MADE UP OF A STAINLESS STEEL ALLOY WITH AN ULTIMATE TENSILE STRENGTH OF OVER 280,000 POUNDS PER SQUARE INCH. THE SAME MATERIAL THEY USE IN LANDING GEAR.
"HE'LL HAVE TO BEND THE METAL SHELL AROUND HIM EVERY TIME HE MAKES A MOVE. THAT SHOULD CUT HIS STRENGTH IN HALF AT THE VERY LEAST.
"IT WON'T HELP HIM FEEL ANYTHING, BUT IT WILL ALLOW HIM TO OPEN A DOOR WITHOUT TEARING IT OFF ITS HINGES."
VEET
FSSSHHHHH
UNFORTUNATELY, HE'LL HAVE TO GO THROUGH THIS PROCESS EVERY TIME HE PUTS ON THE UNIFORM.
T-SPHERES. ACTIVATE THE COOLING JETS.
VEET

HSSSSS
HSSSSS
HSSSSS
FASSSH
SSSSSSS
SSSSSSSS
RAAANK
WHAT...
...DID YOU DO TO ME?

YOU AREN'T IN PAIN, ARE YOU?
NO. NO, I DON'T FEEL A THING.
IT'S THE COLORS.
IT'S IN LINE WITH YOUR GRANDFATHER'S. WE ASSUMED--
YOU SHOULDN'T HAVE.
I DIDN'T WANT A COSTUME, I WANTED SOMETHING THAT WOULD HELP ME.
RAAAK
WE'RE TRYING TO HELP YOU, NATE.
I'M NOT THE "NEW" COMMANDER STEEL, HAWKMAN. I'M NOT EVEN IN THE DAMN MILITARY.
MY UNCLE WAS. AND MY BROTHER...HE COULD'VE BEEN THIS, BUT NOT ME.
IT WASN'T SUPPOSED TO BE ME.
I DON'T KNOW IF I SHOULD BE SALUTING OR SINGING THE AMERICAN ANTHEM.
WOW.
POWER GIRL, THIS IS HARDLY THE TIME.
ACTUALLY IT IS, DOC. THIS MIGHT CONCERN MR. RED, WHITE AND BLUE THERE.
A DOZEN MASKED MEMBERS OF THE AMERICAN SUPREMACIST PARTY HAVE DECIDED TO SUPPORT THE RECENT RISE OF THE FOURTH REICH.
CHECKMATE'S DEALT WITH THE A.S.P. BEFORE.
WE'RE DEALING WITH THESE IGNORANT IDIOTS TODAY.
THEY'RE HOLDING A WORLD CULTURE CLASS AT NYU HOSTAGE. AND THEY'RE DEMANDING THE RELEASE OF CAPTAIN NAZI IN AN HOUR OR THEY START SHOOTING STUDENTS.
THAT MEANS THEY'RE THREATENING KIDS.
YOU IN, HEYWOOD?

AREN'T YOU GOING TO DRINK YOUR MILK?
IT MAKES YOUR BONES STRONGER.
Um, NO.

YOU'RE NOT STILL MAD AT ME, ARE YOU, KAL?
I'M NOT MAD AT YOU, THOM.
THEN WE'RE STILL FRIENDS?
THE LEGION WILL ALWAYS BE MY FRIENDS.

WHY DIDN'T YOU GO BACK WITH THE OTHER LEGIONNAIRES?
HELP WHO?
I WANTED TO, BUT I CAN'T. I'M HERE TO HELP.
MYSELF. AND EARTH, TOO!
THE BLACK HOLE IS SUPPOSED TO HELP HER SEE THE TRUTH. THEN HE'LL COME AND WHY... THE JUSTICE SOCIETY OF AMERICA SHOWS US ALL THE WAY.

THE WORLD NEEDS BETTER GOOD GUYS!
THAT'S NOT JUST OUR WORLD, YOU KNOW. OR OUR TIME.
BUT THE FUTURE ISN'T UP TO ME TO SAVE. I HAVE MY OWN JOB. I HAVE GRAVITY POWERS!

WHEN THEY OPENED THE SPEED FORCE, WALLY WEST AND HIS FAMILY CAME BACK.
AND THEY SAY LIGHTNING NEVER STRIKES TWICE IN THE SAME PLACE! Pfft! JUST ASK HIM.
BUT IS THAT WHY THE LEGION WERE HERE? TO BRING THE FLASH HOME?

FROM THE VIBRATIONAL PLANE! ZIP! ZOOM! THE LEGION OF THREE WORLDS! DO YOU REMEMBER XS?

MINE TOO. I LIKE POWER GIRL AN AWFUL LOT, BUT NOT IN THE WAY I LOVE MY DREAMER.
I CAN'T WAIT TO SEE HER AGAIN.
MILK

CHOMPF

I'M QUITE HAPPY ABOUT *THAT.*
KRNCH!

WHY DID THE LEGION COME BACK HERE?
THERE'S *TROUBLE* IN THE 31ST CENTURY, YOU SEE. THE BIG THREE SAY YOU *CAN'T* HELP THEM.
WHY NOT?
WHY CLARK KENTS CAN'T COME!

IT'S COMMON SENSE.

SHE HAD ***SUCH*** A ***CRUSH*** ON YOU.
AND I GOT TO MEET ANOTHER THOM AND ANOTHER THOM!

I DON'T UNDERSTAND WHAT YOU'RE TALKING ABOUT.

YEAH.
ME EITHER.

NEW YORK UNIVERSITY.
WILDCAT
STARGIRL
POWER GIRL
WILDCAT
DAMAGE
CYCLONE
ALL RIGHT, GANG.
RAANK
RAANK
RAANK
RAANK
ARE YOU ALL RIGHT, NATHAN?
IT'S NATE.
NATE. ARE YOU ALL RIGHT?

THEY'RE FOCUSED ON THE WINDOWS AND DOORS SO IF WE GO THROUGH THAT WALL, WHICH I'M HAPPY TO DO, THEY'LL MOVE THEIR ATTENTION TO US.
X-RAY VISION TELLS ME THERE'S TEN OF THESE GUYS LINED UP TOGETHER RIGHT PAST THAT WALL. STUDENTS ARE HUDDLED IN THE CORNER.
WHERE'S HEYWOOD?
HE'S, uh, HE'S BACK THERE.
MAYBE HE'S NERVOUS.
MAYBE THE TIN MAN NEEDS HIS OIL CAN.
MAYBE HE'S ALLERGIC TO CATS.
WHAP
YOU'RE A FOOTBALL PLAYER, RIGHT?
NO. I HAVEN'T WALKED IN OVER A YEAR. THE WEIGHT OF THIS METAL ON ME MAKES IT IMPOSSIBLE TO RUN. AND I CAN HEAR THE WIND, BUT I CAN'T FEEL IT.
I WAS.
STAY RIGHT HERE. AND CATCH WHAT WE THROW AT YOU.
WHAT ARE YOU GONNA THROW AT ME?

YOU WANT US TO DO WHAT?
PLAY CATCH, DAMAGE.

WHUMP
KA-TING
KA-TING
BRAT-TAT-TAT
FREE CAPTAIN NAZI!
FREE THE WHITE MAN'S *REAL* SUPERMAN!
KRSSHH
THUMP

WHAT IF I MISS, COURT?
YOU'VE BEEN PRACTICING YOUR FUNNELING. YOU WON'T MISS.
BUT WHAT IF I DO?
YOU THROW ANOTHER ONE.
...BUT I DON'T LIKE USING MY FISTS, POP.
FISTS ARE NATURE'S PROBLEM SOLVERS.
ALAN SAYS THAT ABOUT OUR BRAINS.
AND WHAT'S *HAWKMAN* TELL YA?
NOTHIN'. HE JUST *GRUNTS* A LOT. LIKE *DAMAGE.*
SWAGG
C'MERE.
KINGG
KONGG

HN.

BOO TO NAZIS!

KRACKK
HEY, POWER GIRL!
YEAH, NATE?

HOW'D I DO?
PERFECT.

OH, HONEY. I WAS SO WORRIED ABOUT YOU. SO WORRIED.
LOOK FAMILIAR?
FBI
YEAH! LET'S GET A SHOT AT THE NEW COMMANDER STEEL!
COMMANDER STEEL! CAN YOU GIVE ME A *SMILE!*
I'M NOT--
I'M NOT COMMANDER STEEL...I'M JUST-- JUST A GUY.
YOU HEAR THAT? SAYS HE'S A REGULAR OLD "CITIZEN."
HE *IS.*
THIS IS *CITIZEN STEEL.*
THAT NAME *WORK?*
CAN I SEE MY FAMILY NOW?

RAANK RAANK
WE CAN'T ALLOW THIS!
WE CAN'T HAVE THAT KIND OF EXTENSIVE DAMAGE AGAIN. THE DOORS HE TORE APART THE LAST TIME--
ARE BEING PAID FOR BY THE JUSTICE SOCIETY OF AMERICA.
AND YOU CAN EXPECT A LARGE DONATION FROM MR. TERRIFIC TO COVER THE EXPENSES FOR THE HEYWOOD FAMILY.
BUT THE CRACKS IN THE FLOOR--
PLEASE, DOCTOR.
YOU KNOW WHAT THESE KIDS HAVE BEEN THROUGH.
GO AHEAD, NATE.
YOU'RE NOT GOING TO HURT THEM.

RAANK
RAANK
HEY, GUYS.
NATE? NATE, IS THAT YOU?
NATE?
NO WAY! NATE!
HE LOOKS AWESOME!
NATE!
COOL!
NATE!
NATE!
NATE!

IT'S GOOD TO SEE ALL OF YOU.

IT TAKES ME A SECOND TO REALIZE...

...FOR THE FIRST TIME IN A LONG, LONG TIME...

JUSTICE SOCIETY OF AMERICA #8 cover A by ALEX ROSS

JUSTICE SOCIETY OF AMERICA #8 cover B by **DALE EAGLESHAM & RODNEY RAMOS** Interior art by **FERNANDO PASARIN & RAMOS**

MONDAY.
THERE'S DAMAGE.
WHAT A FIRST ASSIGNMENT, *eh,* BABE? TRY AND RECRUIT THE "DYNAMITE" KID.
DID YOU FEED THE METER?
IT'S GOT *TWENTY* MINUTES ON IT.
THAT'S *PLENTY* OF TIME TO GET HIM TO SAY, "YES."

TUESDAY.
OOPS. I THINK WE JUST BROKE HIS ARMS.
KRAKK
TAKE NOTE, DAMAGE. YOU'RE NOT SUPPOSED TO USE EXCESSIVE *FORCE--*
--STARTING *TOMORROW.*

WEDNESDAY.
WELCOME ABOARD, TOMMY!
Um, THANKS, LIBERTY BELLE.
THE BIG BAD CAT HAS A KITTEN!
FORGET THE *MEETING,* THIS CALLS FOR A *PARTY!*

FRIDAY.
KRAKKKOOM
WE CAN CATCH THE FIRST FLIGHT OUT TOMORROW.
SOUNDS GOOD TO ME, BABE.

SATURDAY.
WOOOO HOOOOOO!!
MY NAME'S JESSE CHAMBERS.
THAT'S MY HUSBAND, RICK TYLER.
AS LIBERTY BELLE AND HOURMAN, WE'RE BOTH MEMBERS OF THE JUSTICE SOCIETY OF AMERICA. THAT MEANS WE'RE PART OF THE TEAM THAT HAS TIES TO EVERY MYSTERY-MAN ON THE PLANET.
EVEN SUPERMAN CAME TO OUR WEDDING.
HIS PRESENT WAS A WEEKEND IN ASPEN. PRETTY COOL, huh?
I'D GUESS FROM THE OUTSIDE, MY LIFE MIGHT LOOK PERFECT--
--BUT IT'S NOT.
BELLS & WHISTLES

IT NEVER HAS BEEN.

YOU READY, SWEETIE?

YEAH. I... I'M *REALLY* GONNA DO IT THIS TIME, DAD.

IT'LL BE *PERFECT.*

OKAY, THEN...

RUN!

3X...2...

...SORRY, DAD.
AW, IT'S ALL RIGHT, JESS.
IT TOOK ME YEARS TO ACHIEVE THE KIND OF CONCENTRATION REQUIRED FOR THIS, BUT ONCE I MASTERED THE MATHEMATICAL FORMULA--

3X2(9YZ)4A!

WOOOSHH

--I DISCOVERED MY FULLEST POTENTIAL AS JOHNNY QUICK.
THE FASTEST TICKLER ALIVE!
HAHA HAHA!

I STILL DON'T GET HOW KNOWING THE ANSWER TO A MATH PROBLEM CAN GIVE YOU SUPER-SPEED.
ALGEBRA NEVER MAKES ME ANYTHING BUT BORED.
IT'S NOT THE FORMULA ITSELF, JESSE, IT'S A STATE OF MIND. A MANTRA FOR TAPPING INTO A POWER I BELIEVE YOU POSSESS. JUST LIKE ME--
--AND YOUR MOTHER.
JOHNNY? ARE YOU DOWN HERE? I THOUGHT I HEARD SOMETHING BREAK.

JESSE?

IT'S OKAY, MOM. YOU'VE GOT A WHOLE *BOX* OF THEM!

IT'S *NOT* OKAY, HONEY. IT'S *TUESDAY MORNING.* YOU'RE SUPPOSED TO BE IN SCHOOL.
DAD CALLED IN FOR ME.
DID HE?
I THOUGHT IT WAS A GOOD DAY FOR SOME HOME SCHOOLING.

STOP FILLING HER HEAD WITH THIS STUFF, JOHNNY.

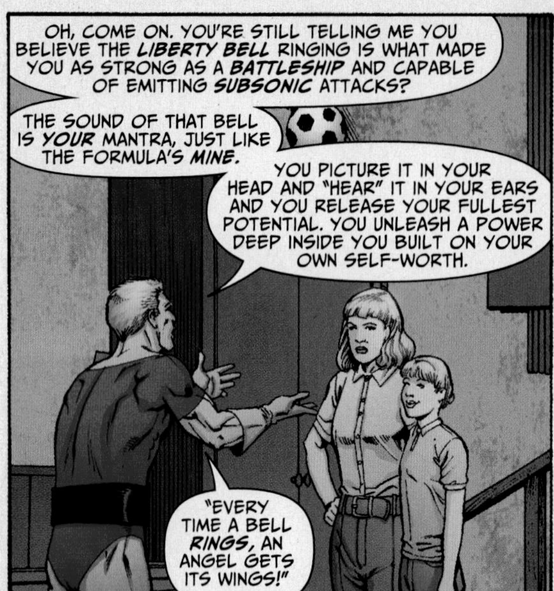
OH, COME ON. YOU'RE STILL TELLING ME YOU BELIEVE THE LIBERTY BELL RINGING IS WHAT MADE YOU AS STRONG AS A BATTLESHIP AND CAPABLE OF EMITTING SUBSONIC ATTACKS?
THE SOUND OF THAT BELL IS YOUR MANTRA, JUST LIKE THE FORMULA'S MINE.
YOU PICTURE IT IN YOUR HEAD AND "HEAR" IT IN YOUR EARS AND YOU RELEASE YOUR FULLEST POTENTIAL. YOU UNLEASH A POWER DEEP INSIDE YOU BUILT ON YOUR OWN SELF-WORTH.
"EVERY TIME A BELL RINGS, AN ANGEL GETS ITS WINGS!"

STOP, JOHNNY. JUST STOP WITH ALL OF THIS NONSENSE!

I'VE NEVER UNDERSTOOD HOW MY POWERS WORK--
I DON'T NEED TO.
YOU SHOULD.
YES, YOU DO.
EVER SINCE THE SQUADRON DISBANDED, YOU'VE BEEN OBSESSED WITH CONVERTING EVERYONE TO YOUR WAY OF THINKING.

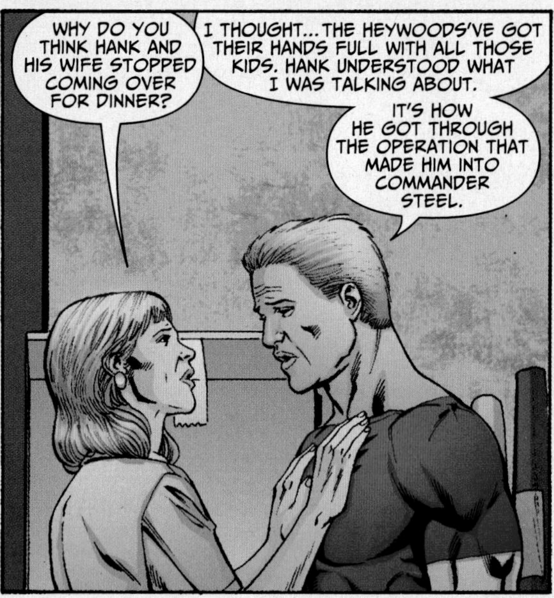
WHY DO YOU THINK HANK AND HIS WIFE STOPPED COMING OVER FOR DINNER?
I THOUGHT... THE HEYWOODS'VE GOT THEIR HANDS FULL WITH ALL THOSE KIDS. HANK UNDERSTOOD WHAT I WAS TALKING ABOUT.
IT'S HOW HE GOT THROUGH THE OPERATION THAT MADE HIM INTO COMMANDER STEEL.

HE WAS BEING NICE, JOHNNY. LIKE ALL OF OUR FRIENDS HAVE TRIED TO BE.
AS MUCH AS YOU COMPLAINED ABOUT MAX MERCURY PUSHING HIS THEORIES OF A "SPEED FORCE" ON TO YOU, THAT'S EXACTLY WHAT YOU'RE DOING TO OUR FRIENDS AND OUR DAUGHTER.

MAX MERCURY'S "SPEED FORCE" IS AN ABSURD CONCEPT, LIBBY. IT'S UNQUANTIFIABLE AND UNPROVEN.
MY FORMULA WORKS.

AND YOU'RE USING OUR DAUGHTER TO PROVE THAT, IS THAT IT? ALL BECAUSE A DOZEN OF THE WORLD'S TOP SCIENTISTS LAUGHED IN YOUR FACE?
I'LL SHOW THEM THEY'RE WRONG.
JESSE HAS THE POTENTIAL TO TAP INTO BOTH OF OUR POWERS. YOUR STRENGTH. MY SPEED.
SHE JUST NEEDS TO FIND HER MANTRA.
RECITING A STRING OF LETTERS AND NUMBERS WON'T MAKE YOU BETTER THAN YOU ALREADY ARE, JESSE--

DON'T YOU TELL HER THAT, LIBBY. DON'T TAKE AWAY HER HOPE TO BECOME SOMETHING SPECIAL.

SHE ALREADY IS SPECIAL, JOHNNY.

JESSE... I...

...I DIDN'T MEAN IT THAT WAY...

IT'S OKAY, DAD.

LESS THAN A YEAR LATER, MY MOM DIVORCED HIM.

I LIVED WITH MY DAD UNTIL I WENT TO COLLEGE.
I DIDN'T GO TO PARTIES. I DIDN'T DATE. I STUDIED. OR I MEDITATED. UNTIL I EVENTUALLY UNLOCKED THE FORMULA. I GOT IT PERFECT.
3X2(9YZ)4A!
THAT'S MY GIRL!
I DIDN'T KNOW HOW OR WHY, BUT I COULD RUN AND FLY AS FAST AS MY DAD.
AND I KNEW WHAT IT MEANT TO HIM THAT I DID.
I WAS DOING A DISSERTATION ON "MYSTERY-MEN AND THEIR EFFECTS ON CULTURE" SO HE HOOKED ME UP WITH AN UNOFFICIAL INTERNSHIP WITH THE JUSTICE SOCIETY.
THAT SUMMER, LIKE THE FORMULA, WAS PERFECT.
AND THAT SUMMER I SWORE MY LIFE WOULD STAY THAT WAY. I CUT EVERYTHING THAT WASN'T PERFECT I CUT OUT OF IT.
The Philadelphia In
INTRODUCING "JESSE" QUICK
HI, JESSE. IT'S, UM, IT'S MOM AGAIN.
I JUST WANTED TO SEE HOW SCHOOL WAS GOING. SO I...
...I HOPE YOU'RE HAVING A GOOD TIME, HONEY. I LOVE--
KLIZZT
IF IT WASN'T PERFECT, IT WASN'T IN MY LIFE.
I DIDN'T WANT MY MOM...OR HER POWERS.
A FEW MONTHS LATER, MY DAD FOUND OUT HIS FORMULA WAS EXACTLY WHAT MOM SAID IT WAS.
HIS POWER AND MINE CAME FROM AN ENERGY CALLED THE "SPEED FORCE."
HE DIED PROTECTING ME FROM A PSYCHOTIC SPEEDSTER OBSESSED WITH CONTROLLING IT.
I GAVE AWAY MY SPEED A YEAR LATER WHEN THE FLASH WENT UP AGAINST ANOTHER LIGHT SPEED SOCIOPATH.
A ROGUE PROFILER NAMED HUNTER ZOLOMON.

HE CALLS HIMSELF ZOOM.
YOU'RE JUST ADDING TO THE LIST OF THINGS YOU HAVE TO ANSWER FOR, HUNTER.
MYJOB'S BEEN GETTING EAAAAASIER, JAYYY.
THANKSTOTHE JUSTICESOCIETY OFAMERICA.
MAKING BETTERRRR HEROES. THAT'S WHATIDOOOTOOO. I PUTTHEMTHROUGH TRAGEDYYYY.
BOOOM
YOU TORTURE THEM, IS WHAT YOU DO.
TOMATO TOMATOEEEEE.
JAY'S BARELY KEEPING UP.
WITH WALLY AND THE SPEED FORCE BACK, HE'S DOING FINE.
WE NEED TO SEND THE KIDS BACK.
WHY?
LOOK UP AHEAD.
WILL YOU SPEED THIS THING UP, STARGIRL?
I WANT IN ON THIS.
WATCH THE BACKSEAT DRIVING, DAMAGE.
HOLD UP, KIDS.

Welcome To
GEORGIA
The Peach State
THIS IS AS FAR AS YOU GO, DAMAGE.
WE'RE AT THE GEORGIA STATE LINE.
I CAN READ, GREEN LANTERN.
THEN YOU KNOW YOUR INVOLVEMENT STOPS HERE. I'M SORRY, SON.
YOU KNOW WHAT ZOOM DID TO ME.
AND YOU KNOW WHAT YOU DID TO ATLANTA.
YEAH.
I KNOW.
KRAKL
BOOOM
WOW! LOOK AT HIM LEAP! I DIDN'T KNOW HE COULD DO THAT. DID YOU KNOW HE COULD DO THAT?
THAT ISN'T GOOD, CYCLONE.
WHY NOT?
BECAUSE HE MADE A PROMISE TO THE STATE OF GEORGIA. HE SWORE HE'D NEVER STEP OVER THE STATE LINE, AND THEY AGREED NOT TO CHARGE HIM.
CHARGE HIM? FOR WHAT?
WHEN HE FIRST STARTED OUT, HE LOST CONTROL OF HIS POWERS--

"--AND HE BLEW UP HALF OF DOWNTOWN ATLANTA."

RICK'S TALKED THE LIFE STORY OUT OF OUR WAITER BEFORE WE EVEN ORDER.
...FROM OMAHA? I STOPPED THE ICICLE FROM FREEZING THE FIELDS OUT THERE ONCE. BEAUTIFUL CITY. YOU STILL HAVE FAMILY THERE?

HE BUYS A BOTTLE OF CHAMPAGNE FOR THE COUPLE CELEBRATING THEIR TWENTIETH ANNIVERSARY NEXT TO US.
CONGRATULATIONS! HERE'S TO TWENTY MORE!

AND HE OFFERS TO HELP THE BUSBOY WHO'S WORKING HIS WAY THROUGH ARCHITECTURE CLASSES.
...GIVE JOHN STEWART A CALL AND SEE WHAT I CAN FIND OUT ABOUT STUDENT-MENTOR PROGRAMS.
THAT'D BE GREAT, MR. TYLER.

ONCE IN AWHILE, WE'LL GET A FEW LOOKS WHEN HE LAUGHS TOO LOUD OR COMES ON TOO STRONG.
WHEN I FIRST MET RICK, I THOUGHT HE WAS RUDE, OBNOXIOUS AND OBVIOUSLY OVERCOMPENSATING.
I DIDN'T REALIZE WHY HE WAS ALWAYS SMILING, BUT I SHOULD'VE.

I WAS TOO CAUGHT UP IN MYSELF TO PUT TWO AND TWO TOGETHER.
THAT SAME DAY I SAW SOMETHING IN RICK, HE SHOWED ME SOMETHING I'D NEVER SEEN IN THE LIBERTY BELL BEFORE.
THAT BELL BECAME EVERYTHING TO ME.
WHAT?
IT BECAME MY MANTRA.
NOTHING.
EXCUSE ME, MRS. CHAMBERS.

DO YOU MIND SIGNING THIS FOR US?
OH. I HAVEN'T SEEN THIS ONE.
LET ME SEE!

BRIDES
MONTHLY
WEDDING COSTUMES
SUPER-HERO WEDDING!
HOW TO MARRY A
SUPER-HERO

VEET
VEET

HELLO?

JESSE? RICK?
I HATE TO BOTHER YOU TWO IN THE MIDDLE OF YOUR TRIP...
WHAT'S UP, POWER GIRL?
THE JUSTICE LEAGUE HAD A RUN-IN WITH ZOOM A FEW DAYS AGO IN KEYSTONE. WE WERE "LUCKY" AND WE CAUGHT UP WITH HIM.
ZOOM?
WE'VE BEEN CHASING HIM FOR THE LAST HOUR.
IS GRANT THERE?

...YEAH. DAMAGE FOLLOWED HIM RIGHT INTO ATLANTA. HE AND ZOOM WENT AT IT.

WE KNOW, JESSE. WE TRIED TO TELL HIM. NOW WE'VE GOT A HOSTAGE SITUATION.

ATLANTA? GRANT CAN'T--

ZOOM HAS DAMAGE HOSTAGE?

POLICE

TRY THE OTHER WAY AROUND.

THE FLASH IS GOING TO FIND YOUR PARENTS, THEN WE'LL GET YOU OUT OF HERE, OKAY?
THERE'S ROOM FOR EVERYONE! PLEASE STOP PUSHING!
WE NEED TO CLEAR THE STREETS! THESE BUSES HAVE TO ROLL NOW!
82

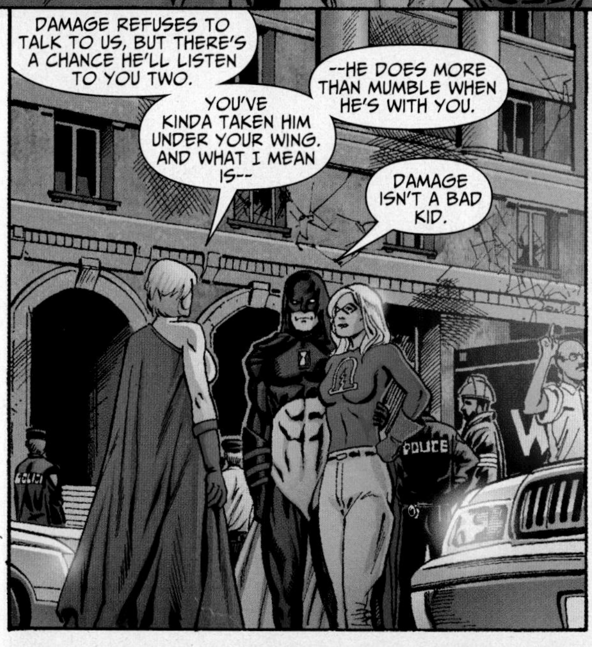
DAMAGE REFUSES TO TALK TO US, BUT THERE'S A CHANCE HE'LL LISTEN TO YOU TWO.
--HE DOES MORE THAN MUMBLE WHEN HE'S WITH YOU.
YOU'VE KINDA TAKEN HIM UNDER YOUR WING. AND WHAT I MEAN IS--
DAMAGE ISN'T A BAD KID.
POLICE

I KNOW HE'S NOT, HOURMAN, BUT THIS ISN'T JUST ABOUT HIM.
DAMAGE WAS "OUTLAWED" IN THIS STATE BECAUSE HE BLEW UP HALF OF DOWNTOWN ATLANTA BY ACCIDENT.
THIS TIME THE CITY HASN'T BEEN FULLY EVACUATED YET. AND THIS TIME, HE COULD DO SOMETHING ON PURPOSE.

IF HIS FUSE LIGHTS, WE'RE TALKING HUNDREDS OF THOUSANDS. MINIMUM.

I'LL GO.

HON, LET ME COME--
I DON'T WANT TO OVERWHELM GRANT. I'M SURE HIS HEAD IS SPINNING AS IT IS.
YOU HELP THE OTHERS WITH THE EVACUATION. KEEP A SAFE DISTANCE.
WAT

I DON'T LIKE THIS.
ZOOM'S IN THERE TOO, BABE. AND YOU'RE NOT *JESSE QUICK* ANYMORE.
I CAN HANDLE GRANT.

I KNOW.

POLICE

I LOVE YOU.

I LOVE YOU TOO.

LIBERTY BELLE?
JESSE CHAMBERS. FLASHWANNABE.
SHUT.
UP.

THIS ISN'T THE WAY TO DEAL WITH ZOOM.

YOU KNOW WHAT HE DID TO MY FACE.

YOUR FACE ISN'T WHO YOU ARE.

I'M A HORROR SHOW UNDER HERE. I...
...I BROKE EVERY MIRROR IN MY APARTMENT. I CAN'T LOOK IN THEM.
I KNOW I'M NEVER GOING TO BE WITH A GIRL AGAIN, JESSE. NO ONE'S EVER GOING TO STOMACH WHAT I AM.

I'VE BUILT UP ENOUGH ENERGY INSIDE, YOU MOVE ME AT ALL, YOU EVEN VIBRATE OUT OF MY GRIP--
--AND IT'LL BE LIKE PULLING A PIN FROM A GRENADE.
BEFORE I WORETHISUNIFORMI WAS A POLICE PROFILER. IIIIII STUDIEDTHE FLASH'S ROGUES.
THEY'RE MORECOMPLICATED THAN MOOOOSSSTTT PEOPLETHINK.
SO ARE YOU.
"I TOLD YOU THAT WHENIBROKETHEFREEDOM FIGHTERSANDYOURFACE."
"DO YOU REMEMBER?"
"TODAY, HOWEVER, YOU MUST KNOW WHAT THECOSTOFYOUR REVENGGGGGGEEEEEEE IS."
I DON'T UNDERSTAND WHAT YOU'RE SAYING.
I TOLD YOU YOU WOULD BEEEE A STRONNNNNGER HERO IFYOUSURVIVED.
YOUEXPLODE YOUKILLMEYOUKILLYOU ANDYOUKILLTHOUSANDS MORE.
NOTHING YOU SAY MATTERS TO ME, ZOOM.
THEN LISTEN TO ME, DAMAGE.

WHEN CAPTAIN NAZI RIPPED OFF YOUR MASK, I SAW YOUR FACE.
WHAT DID *I* DO?
YOU'RE DIFFERENT.
I'M NOT AS DIFFERENT AS YOU THINK.
YES, YOU ARE. YOU AND HOURMAN. YOU'RE LIKE THIS *PERFECT* COUPLE. ALWAYS LAUGHING AND SMILING.
I WASN'T PERFECT WHEN I LOST MY SPEED--

YOU DIDN'T *LOSE* IT, JESSE. YOU FELTUNWORTHY.
YOU GAVE THEMTOTHEFLASH AND SEVEREDYOUR CONNECTION WITH THE SPEED FORCE.

YOU LEAVE HER ALONE OR I'LL--

IT'S OKAY, GRANT. IT'S OKAY.
AS BACKWARDS AS IT IS, ZOOM'S RIGHT ABOUT ME.

AFTER MY DAD DIED, I DIDN'T WANT TO BE JESSE QUICK ANYMORE. I DIDN'T FEEL I DESERVED IT.
I GAVE *UP* MY SPEED. I GAVE UP WEARING A MASK.
MY MOM CONFRONTED ME AT THE BROWNSTONE A FEW MONTHS LATER. WANTING TO KNOW WHY I QUIT. IF SHE COULD HELP.
RICK HEARD US ARGUING. HE HEARD ME SAY SOME PRETTY AWFUL THINGS TO HER.
HE ASKED ME WHY I WAS SO HARD ON HER. AND WHY I WAS SO HARD ON MYSELF.

I WAS ALWAYS STRIVING TO BE PERFECT. I EXPECTED EVERYONE ELSE TO BE PERFECT TOO.
RICK DIDN'T UNDERSTAND WHY.
HE DREW THIS ON A PIECE OF PAPER. AND HE SAID...

..."JUST BECAUSE SOMETHING HAS A CRACK IN IT DOESN'T MEAN YOU THROW IT AWAY."
THAT BECAME MY NEW MANTRA. AND MY DAD WAS RIGHT...ALL THE POWERS MY MOTHER HAD, I DID TOO.

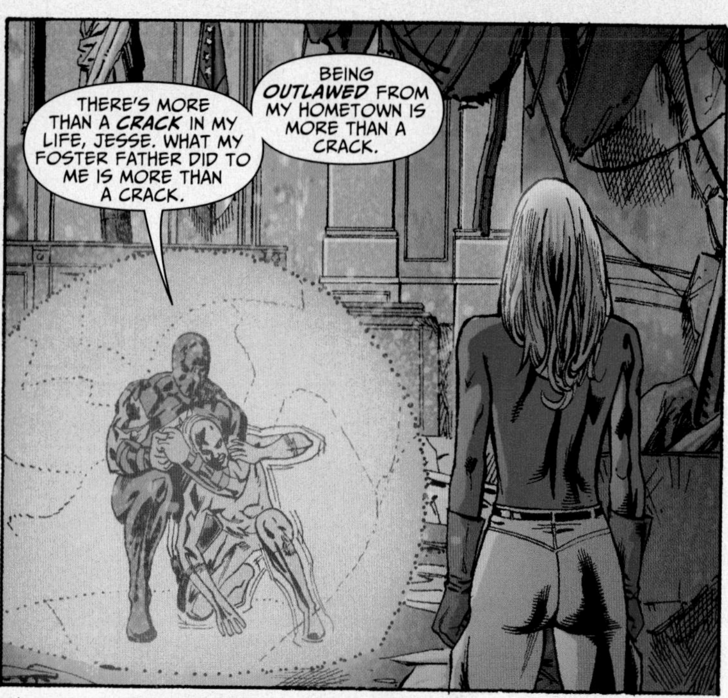
BEING OUTLAWED FROM MY HOMETOWN IS MORE THAN A CRACK.
THERE'S MORE THAN A CRACK IN MY LIFE, JESSE. WHAT MY FOSTER FATHER DID TO ME IS MORE THAN A CRACK.

THIS IS MORE THAN A CRACK.

IT DOESN'T HAVE TO BE. IT REALLY DOESN'T.

YOUSHUTHIMDOWN.

KRANKK

YOU'RE TOOSOFT ON HIMMMMM JESSSSEEEE.

LIKEWALLYWEST HE NEEDS TRAGEDYYYYYY TO OVERCOME. HEDOESN'T NEEDABIGSISTERRRRR.

DAMAGE WILL NEVER SUCCEED. HE'S A FAILURE LIKE YOUUUUU TO YOURFATHER.

I'M PUTTINGHIMOUT OF HIS MISERY.

AND YOU'RE **NEXT.**

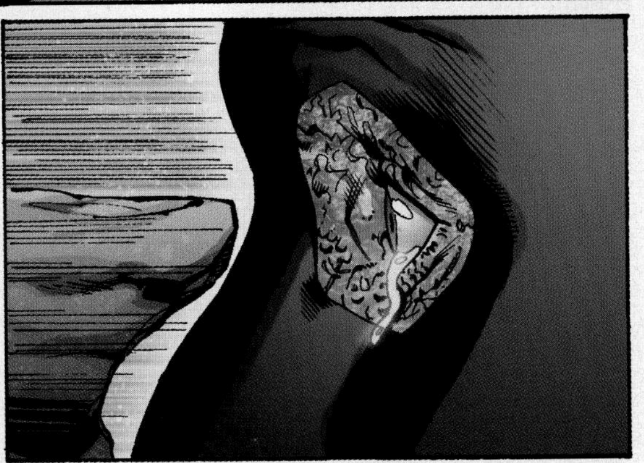

3X2(9YZ)4A!
KKTCH
FZZCH

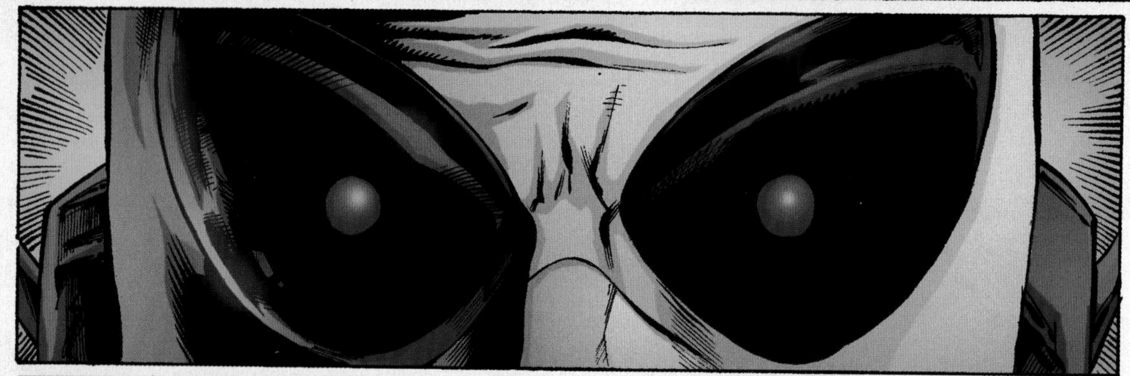

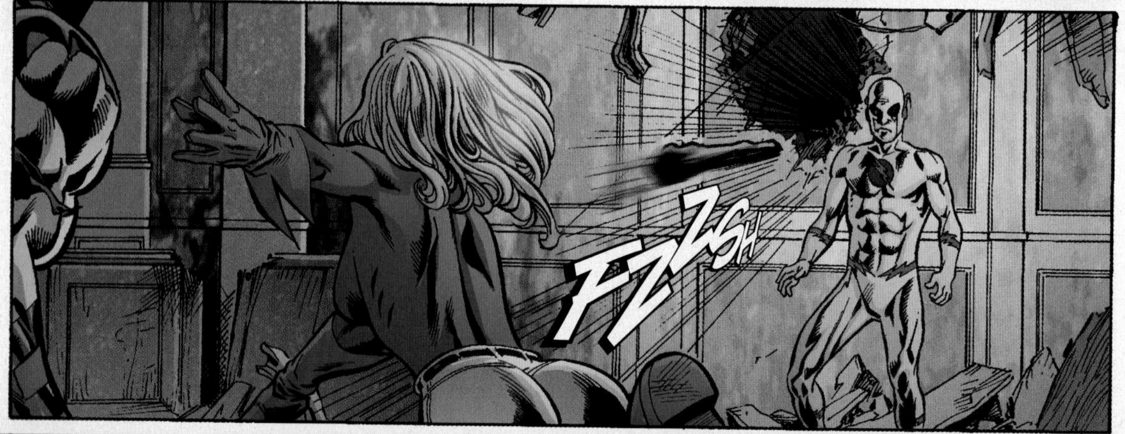
FZZSH

KRAKK

THAT WAS...
Y-YEAH.
AWESOME?
I THOUGHT YOU SAID YOU DIDN'T DESERVE THE SPEED.
I GOT OVER IT.
HOLD IT!
DON'T MOVE!
GRANT EMERSON. YOU'VE VIOLATED THE LEGAL AGREEMENT BETWEEN YOU AND THE STATE OF GEORGIA.
WE'RE PLACING YOU UNDER ARREST.
WITH ALL DUE RESPECT, OFFICER...
...YOU ARREST HIM, YOU ARREST ME.
NO.

YOU ARREST DAMAGE...
...YOU ARREST ALL OF US.

YOU READY TO GO HOME, HON?
HOME?
I'VE GOT A BETTER IDEA.

SUNDAY.
MY LIFE'S GREAT, BUT IT'S NOT PERFECT.
WOO-HOO!
NOBODY IN MY LIFE IS PERFECT.
POWER GIRL-- LOOK OUT! IT'S AN AVALANCHE!
HAHA HAHA!
AND NOBODY HAS TO BE.

JUSTICE SOCIETY OF AMERICA #9 cover A by ALEX ROSS

JUSTICE SOCIETY OF AMERICA #9 cover B and interior art by DALE EAGLESHAM & RUY JOSÉ

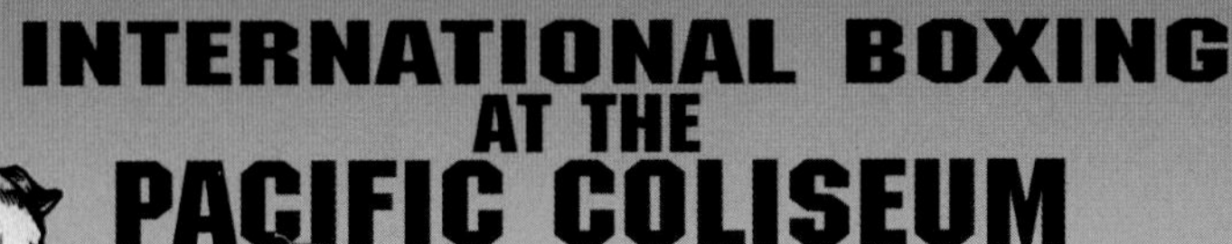

ON THE UNDERCARD:
GENTLEMAN GEOFF JOHNS VS DANGEROUS DALE EAGLESHAM
RAZOR RUY JOSE VS JACKHAMMER JEROMY COX

- EXHIBITION FIGHT - PROCEEDS FOR CHARITY -

BROOKLYN, NY - SEPTEMBER 2007

A MILLION DOLLAR FISTIC CLASSIC

THY KINGDOM COME
MY NAME IS POWER GIRL.
I'M THE LAST DAUGHTER OF THE MULTIVERSE.
I WAS BORN IN A PARALLEL UNIVERSE ON A PARALLEL KRYPTON.
MY COUSIN, KAL-L, AND I WERE THAT KRYPTON'S ONLY SURVIVORS.
YEARS AGO, MY UNIVERSE WAS ANNIHILATED. ALONG WITH AN INFINITE NUMBER OF PARALLEL UNIVERSES.
UNTIL THERE WAS ONLY ONE UNIVERSE LEFT. ONE EARTH.
I WAS FOUND BY THIS EARTH'S SUPERMAN AND WELCOMED INTO THE JUSTICE SOCIETY OF AMERICA.
ALL THE WHILE, I THOUGHT MY COUSIN, THE ONLY FAMILY I'D EVER HAD, WAS DEAD.
I WAS WRONG.
HERE LIES
KAL-L
IT'S NOT GOING TO END.

IT'S NEVER GOING TO END... FOR US...
KAL-L?!
...ONE DAY YOU'LL SEE...
WHAT I SEE ISN'T A DREAM.
IT'S A PREMONITION.
...THEY'RE STILL OUT THERE...
SUPERMAN?
KAL-L WASN'T DEAD. HE WAS LOST IN LIMBO.
BUT HE BROKE FREE FROM THE PRISON HE WAS TRAPPED IN.
AND HE LOOKED DOWN AT THIS LAST SURVIVING EARTH WITH DISAPPOINTMENT.
AL-L DIED REMINDING US THAT IT ISN'T ABOUT OUR POWERS OR HAT WE WEAR ON OUR CHEST.
IT'S ABOUT WHAT WE DO.
IT'S ABOUT ACTION.
THE WORLD NEEDED BETTER GOOD GUYS.
I ACCEPTED THE ROLE AS CHAIRWOMAN OF THE JUSTICE SOCIETY OF AMERICA TO KEEP KAL-L'S DREAM ALIVE.
MEOWWW
BUT THERE'S NOT A MOMENT THAT I DON'T MISS HIM.
AND THAT I DON'T HOPE THAT HIS LAST WORDS MEAN THAT SOMEHOW, SOME WAY--
--SUPERMAN WILL RETURN.

BROOKLYN.
THE KIDS LOVE THAT PICTURE...
146
146
146
146

POWER GIRL
Kara Zor-L. Kryptonian survivor from a parallel universe.
GREEN LANTERN
Alan Scott. Keeper of the Green Flame.
THE FLASH
Jay Garrick. The original fastest man alive.
...AND THE NEW FIRE ENGINE, OF COURSE.
IT'S OUR WAY OF APOLOGIZING FOR WILDCAT. HE DOESN'T USUALLY THROW OUR ADVERSARIES INTO ONCOMING TRAFFIC.
TO BE HONEST, THE CREW LOVED IT. CHANCE OF A LIFETIME TO HELP A WORLD CHAMPION WITH A KNOCKOUT.
UNCLE NATE? UNCLE NATE?!
LIBERTY BELLE
Jesse Chambers. All-American powerhouse.
HOURMAN
Rick Tyler Super-strength an hour at a time.
DAMAGE
Grant Emerson. Human bomb.

cowboy from the future.
SHE'S SO CUTE.
NO.
BUT, HONEY--
NO.
...IT DOESN'T REALLY MAKE SENSE. NOT THAT YOU DON'T MAKE SENSE, WELL, SOMETIMES YOU DON'T. I CAN'T BELIEVE YOU NEVER HAD MAPLE SYRUP!
OF COURSE I'VE HAD MAPLE SYRUP, MAXINE, BUT ON PANCAKES?!
AND YOU THINK I'M ODD.
SIGLAIN
THAT'S DAMAGE.
HE'S NOT ALLOWED TO GO TO ATLANTA, BUT HE WENT ANYWAY. AND HE TOOK DOWN ZOOM! HE'S BAD ASS.
I BET HE COULD BEAT UP SUPERMAN.
COULD YOU BEAT UP SUPERMAN?
LET YOU GUYS IN ON A SECRET. I COULD BEAT UP THE WHOLE JUSTICE LEAGUE.
WOW.
KNEWIT.
STARGIRL
Courtney Whitmore.
Star-powered teenager.
CYCLONE
Maxine Hunkel.
Teenaged wind witch.
CITIZEN STEEL
Nate Heywood.
Indestructible Man.

UNCLE NATE! WE NEED MORE PANCAKES!
FRESH DOLLARS COMIN' RIGHT--
UNCLE NATE, JACK'S SQUIRTIN' SYRUP AT ME!
JACK, STOP WITH THE SYRUP!
KEITH STARTED IT! HE THREW FLOUR IN MY FACE!
DON'T WASTE ANY MORE FLOUR! WE'RE ALMOST OUT OF PANCAKE BATTER!
NICOLE, GET AMANDA AND JORDAN OFF THOSE SHELVES!
HEY, UNCLE NATE!
I JUST MADE THE BIGGEST PANCAKE IN THE WORLD!
AND THEY THINK FIGHTING NAZIS IS HARD.
WHERE'S THE FIRE

RANK RANK RANK
WHO'S STILL HUNGRY?
FONY
FIRE
JOHNNY
YOU'RE A BIT OLD FOR HER, AREN'T YOU, SON?
OH, *uh*, MR. GARRICK, SIR. I'M... A BIG FAN, THAT'S ALL.
BIG FAN OF YOU **TOO**. YOU BEING SO ***FAST*** AND, *um...*
YOU HAVE A FIRE TO PUT OUT.
YES, SIR.
JAAAY. I THOUGHT YOU OFFERED TO CLEAR THE TABLES.
I THOUGHT YOU AND MAXINE COULD HELP.
YAY.
HEY, EVERYBODY. YOU MIGHT WANT TO GET OUT HERE.
THE FIGHT'S ABOUT TO START.

DINGGG
THE BRAVEST OF THE BRAVE

I CAN'T BELIEVE YOU TALKED ME INTO THIS.
DON'T GET YOUR TAIL IN A BUNCH, KID.
EGERLAST
NG I O.146
14
I DON'T *LIKE* FIGHTING. *ESPECIALLY* FOR EXHIBITION.
IT'S NOT FER EXHIBITION, KID.
WHAP
IT'S FER CHARITY.
WELL...
...IF IT'S FOR CHARITY...

RRRRAOWWW
C'MON, TED!
C'MON, TOMMY!
YER TELEGRAPHIN' EVERY LEAP WITH THAT TAIL A' YERS.
NO, I'M NOT.
WHAP
WHAP
YES, YA **ARE**.

YOU CHEAT.
WHAT DO YA THINK SUPER-VILLAINS DO?
THEY'LL GO ON AND ON ABOUT THEIR MASTER PLANS AND THEIR PISS-POOR REASONS. THEY'LL GET YA TA LISTEN ABOUT THEIR SAD LITTLE CHILDHOOD--
--JUST TA GET YOUR GUARD DOWN.
STAYIN' IN THE RING IS A MUST TOO.
KRAKK
YOU'RE OLD AND FUNNY.
ISN'T HE ADORABLE?!
HE REMINDS ME OF MY OWN PRECIOUS--TINKERBELL.
TINKERBELL?
I LIKE IT.
BRRRRINNGGGGG
29
WE'LL DRIVE.
OFFICIAL SCORE CARD FOR BOXING
10 POINT MUST
PLACE: ENGINE 146 FIREHOUSE
1 2 3 4 5
BOXER
WILDCAT 1 10
WILDCAT 2 0

.D.N.Y.
40

BROOKLYN

"WHAT DO WE GOT?"
"FIVE-ALARM FIRE AT A PAINT FACTORY.
"ONE UNIT IS ALREADY ON THE SCENE. THEY'RE MISSING TEN FIREMEN WHO WENT INSIDE BEFORE THE FRONT ENTRANCE COLLAPSED."
LYN PAINTS
F.D.N
THIS IS TERRIBLE.
CYCLONE. STICK WITH ME.
WE'RE GOING TO MAKE SOME SMALL TWISTERS TOGETHER. TRY AND DAMPEN THE FIRE WITHOUT SPREADING IT.
OKAY.
NATE, YOU NEED TO STAY HERE.
WHAT? WHY?
RANK
RANK
EVEN IF YOU FOUND ONE OF THESE TRAPPED FIREMEN, YOUR METAL UNIFORM IS GOING TO GET WAY TOO HOT TO TOUCH THEM.
AND YOU'RE GOING TO BE TOO SLOW TO GET THEM OUT.

BWUL
OOSHH
DAD, OVER HERE!
YOU SURE, KID?
I CAN SMELL THEM!
KRRANKK
LOOK OUT!
FWATCH
DON'T WORRY, GUYS.
WE'RE GONNA GET YOU OUTTA HERE.
WHAT DO YOU THINK, ALAN? ARSON? AN ACCIDENT?

OH MY GOD.
DAMAGE AND I TANGLED WITH HIM A FEW YEARS AGO WHEN WE WERE WITH THE TITANS.
GOTH WAS A SINGER. HE LURED KIDS "BACKSTAGE" TO HIS OWN PERSONAL TORTURE CHAMBERS.
THE FREAK CLAIMED HE WAS SOME KINDA DEMON.
THAT'S... THAT'S GOTH, ISN'T IT, JESS?
GOTH? WHO'S GOTH?
LIAR, LIAR, THIS FACTORY'S ON FIRE!
WHOEVER OR WHATEVER GOTH IS, HE'S DEAD.
THE FIRE'S COMING FROM INSIDE HIM-- FROM THAT HOLE HE HAS BLASTED THROUGH HIS CHEST.
GOTH WAS MURDERED.

BWOOOSHH

I CAN FEEL THE HEAT FROM HIS BODY THROUGH THE GREEN FLAME. THE KIND OF ENERGY IT'S UNLEASHING...

...IT'S ACTUALLY AFFECTING MY *RING*.

WHATEVER POWER GOTH POSSESSED IS ABOUT TO ERUPT.

THEN MOVE ASIDE, ALAN. I'LL GRAB HIS BODY AND THROW IT INTO ORBIT--

KAREN, GET BACK. YOUR *SKIN*.

I CAN GET RID OF THE FURNACE BEFORE IT GOES BA-BA-**BOOM!**
STARMAN--
MY LEGION RING PROTECTS ME FROM THE COLD OF SPACE AND THE HEAT OF THE SUN.
AND, WHY, WHENEVER I **REALLY** NEED TO THROW SOMETHING FAR, FAR AWAY, SOMEWHERE WHERE **NOTHING** GETS OUT...
...I THINK OF A **BLACK HOLE.**

HAVE YOU EVER DONE ANYTHING LIKE THAT?
NO, BUT I **CAN** MAKE A BLACK HOLE.
I **KNOW** I CAN.

YOU'RE NOT GONNA LEAVE THIS UP TO CUCKOO-FOR-COCOA-PUFFS, ARE YOU?

ALAN--?
YOU'RE CHAIRWOMAN. IT'S YOUR CALL.

EVERYONE **OUT.**
LET STARMAN DO HIS THING.
BWOOOOSSHHH

MY THING.
LET'S FIND A CENTER MASS.
OH. YOU'LL DO.
NnFff.
KEEP THE VOICES QUIET.
FWP
RRMMBLLL
PLEASE BE QUIET.
PLEASE.

ARGGGHHHH!!

BOOM
STARMAN!

NK.
GONE... THREW HIM AWAY... GOT TO CLOSE... CLOSE THE...

FWOOSH

Nnnn...
...STARMAN?

HE PUT THE *WHOLE* FIRE OUT.

I THINK I SEE HIM!

WHERE...?

...WHERE AM I?

JUSTICE SOCIETY OF AMERICA #10 cover B by **DALE EAGLESHAM & RUY JOSÉ** Interior art by **EAGLESHAM, JOSÉ & DREW GERACI**

JUSTICE SOCIETY OF AMERICA #10 cover A by ALEX ROSS

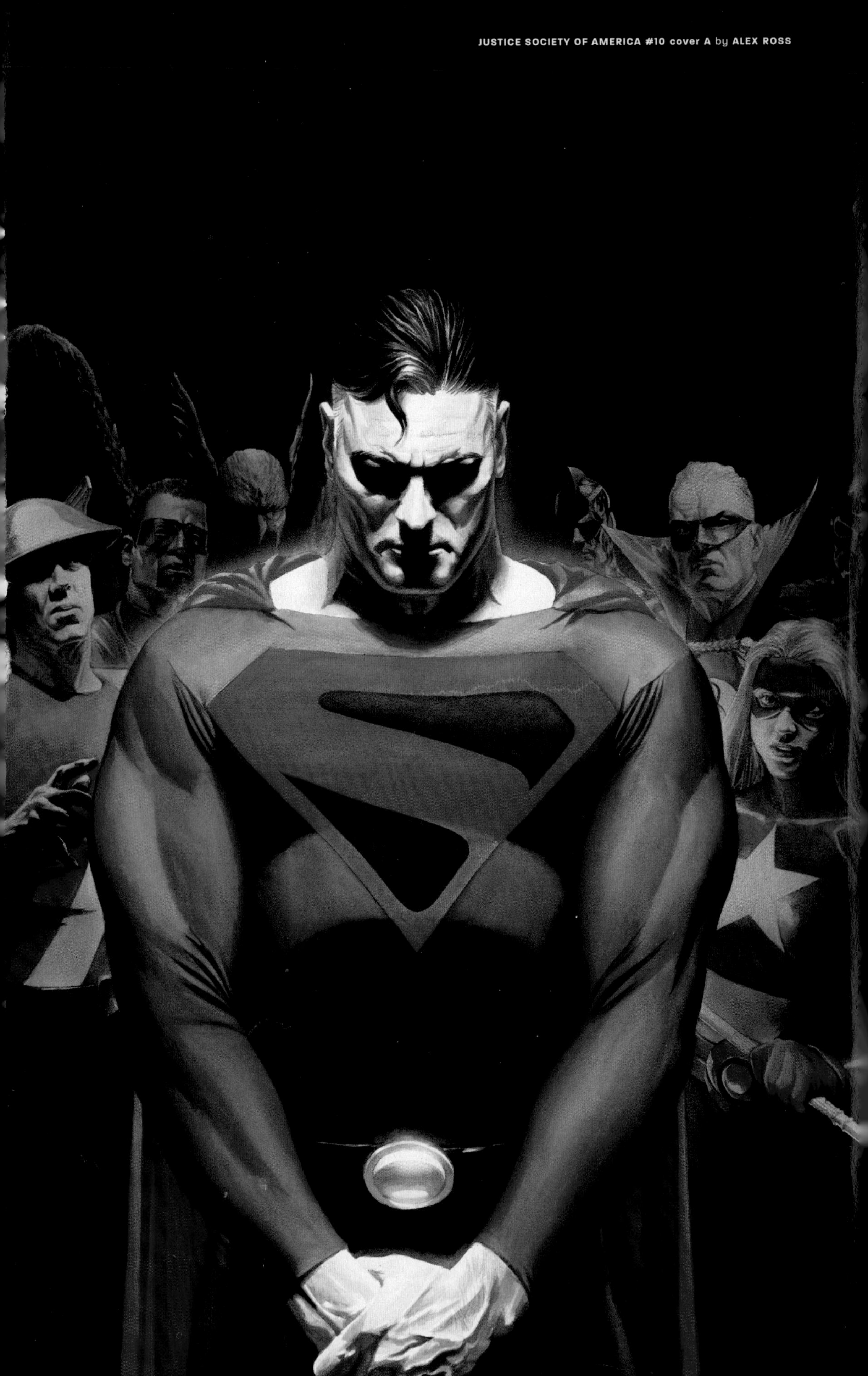

BATTERY PARK, NEW YORK.
HEADQUARTERS OF THE JUSTICE SOCIETY OF AMERICA.
WHOEVER HE IS, POWER GIRL--
--HE'S NOT YOUR COUSIN.
WHAT a WONDERFUL WORLD

POWER GIRL
Kara Zor-L. Kryptonian survivor from a parallel universe.
GREEN LANTERN
Alan Scott. Keeper of the Green Flame.
THE FLASH
Jay Garrick. The original Fastest Man Alive.
WILDCAT
Ted Grant. Former heavyweight champion.
LIBERTY BELLE
Jesse Chambers. All-American powerhouse.
HOURMAN
Rick Tyler. Super-strength an hour at a time.
DAMAGE
Grant Emerson. Human bomb.
STARMAN
Thom Kallor. Unbalanced cosmic cowboy from the future.

BUT THERE AREN'T ANY PARALLEL UNIVERSES. THEY WERE ALL WIPED OUT.
ALONG WITH PRIME, YOU'RE THE LAST SURVIVOR OF THE MULTIVERSE, RIGHT, POWER GIRL?
I THOUGHT SO.
A PARALLEL EARTH? IT SEEMS IMPOSSIBLE, BUT...
I *DO* RECOGNIZE YOU, GREEN LANTERN. YOU'RE YOUNGER, AND YOU'RE WEARING YOUR OLD UNIFORM, BUT YOU'RE STILL ALAN SCOTT.
WILDCAT. THE FLASH. HAWKMAN. POWER WOMAN.
AND RED TORNADO.
POWER *WOMAN?*
RED TORNADO? MY, *uh*, MY NAME'S CYCLONE.
IT'S NICE TO MEET YOU, THOUGH. UNLESS WE *DID* MEET AND I DON'T REMEMBER, THOUGH I THINK I WOULD... MEETING AN OLDER SUPERMAN... FROM A PARALLEL EARTH...
...I THINK I NEED A GLASS OF WATER, GRANDMA.
ON MY EARTH, THE JUSTICE SOCIETY DISBANDED YEARS AGO.
AND THEY *NEVER* REFORMED.
WHY?

DAILY PLANET
MAGOG ACQUITTED
"Justice Done"
CAN I HAVE SOME MORE TEA?

I'LL GET SOME.
EVERYONE, I'D LIKE TO CLEAR THE ROOM. GIVE... SUPERMAN HERE SOME TIME TO CATCH HIS BREATH.
SEE YOU LATER!
KLIK
WHAT ARE YOU DOING, HAWKMAN?
KLANK
SETTING THE SECURITY CODE.
I'M LOCKING HIM IN.

BUT HE HASN'T DONE ANYTHING WRONG, HAS HE?
WE'RE JUST BEING CAUTIOUS, MAXINE.
THE LAST TIME AN "OLDER SUPERMAN" APPEARED ON EARTH, THE UNIVERSE WENT TO HELL.
IT WASN'T KAL-L'S FAULT. IT WAS PRIME.
WE KNOW THAT, COURTNEY.
IT ISN'T ABOUT WHAT THIS SUPERMAN WANTS, BUT WHAT HIS APPEARANCE MEANS.
I HAVE A FEELING THAT EVEN AFTER EVERYTHING WE'VE BEEN THROUGH--
--IT'S NOT QUITE OVER.
I'M CALLING BLACK CANARY. I WANT THE JUSTICE LEAGUE IN ON THIS.
I WANT TO KNOW WHO "SUPERMAN" REALLY IS, WHY HE'S HERE, AND WHAT HE WANTS.
NOT TA POINT OUT THE OBVIOUS, BUT ALL OF YOU DO REALIZE--

"--HE CAN HEAR US."
THEY'RE FRIGHTENED.
SOMETIMES THEY GET FRIGHTENED EASILY.
I DON'T.

YOU'RE ALAN SCOTT'S SON. WEAVER OF THE SHADOW-LANDS.
OBSIDIAN.
YOU RECOGNIZE ME, TOO?
ON... MY EARTH, YOU AND YOUR SISTER TRIED TO HELP REIN IN THE SUPER-POWERED MANIACS. SOME OF THEM WERE SLANDERING THE LEGACIES OF OTHER HEROES LIKE MR. TERRIFIC AND THE STAR-SPANGLED KID.
YOU WERE ON A LEAGUE LED BY BATMAN.
HERE, I'M A MEMBER OF THE JUSTICE SOCIETY OF AMERICA.
IT'S A BIG TEAM.
IT'S MORE THAN A TEAM. IT'S EXACTLY WHAT IT'S CALLED.
A SOCIETY.
IS THAT WHY I DON'T SEE MEN AND WOMEN TOSSING ONE ANOTHER THROUGH BUILDINGS?
OR UNLEASHING LIGHTNING THROUGH THE HEARTS OF THEIR ADVERSARIES?
OR FIELDS SMOLDERING WITH ATOMIC RADIATION FROM A BATTLE THAT WENT TOO FAR?
JOKER
THE JUSTICE SOCIETY IS STILL ACTIVE TO MAKE SURE NO ONE MAKES MISTAKES.
NO. WE'RE HERE TO HELP THEM LEARN FROM THEIR MISTAKES.
NO ONE'S PERFECT.
NO EARTH WILL EVER BE.
AT LEAST THIS ONE IS TRYING.

BROOKLYN.
THE BLACK HOLE STARMAN MANIFESTED DISSIPATED THE ENERGY FROM GOTH'S BODY AS IT DETONATED.
IF IT WEREN'T FOR HIM, ALL OF BROOKLYN MIGHT LOOK LIKE THIS.
THE FIRE DESTROYED ANY TRACE EVIDENCE SURROUNDING GOTH'S MURDER.
WITH HIS BODY INCINERATED, THE ONLY THING WE HAVE TO GO BY IS WHAT LIBERTY BELLE AND THE OTHERS REPORTED SEEING.
A HOLE BLOWN THROUGH HIS TORSO.
NOBODY'S GOING TO BE CRYING OVER A DEAD CHILD KILLER WHO FEIGNED GODHOOD, MID-NITE.
THEN MAYBE THE QUESTION WE SHOULD ASK, MICHAEL--
--IS WHO WOULD BE SMILING OVER THIS?
FAIRPLAY
Terrific
NnkGg.
MID-NITE?
ARE YOU ALL RIGHT?
MUST BE...
...THE SMOKE.
WE BETTER MAKE SURE.

DON'T BLAME THE OTHERS FOR LOCKING YOU IN. THEY'RE BEING CAUTIOUS.
YOU TOLD THEM YOU WATCHED THEM DIE.
ON MY EARTH, YOU DIED TOO.
AND IT WASN'T LEX LUTHOR OR THE ULTRA-HUMANITE OR THAT LAUGHING *PSYCHOPATH* WHO STARTED IT ALL--
--IT WAS THE PEOPLE WE SWORE TO *PROTECT.*
THERE WAS A BREAKOUT AT THE GULAG WHERE WE IMPRISONED THE RECKLESS AND DANGEROUS. WE WERE TRYING TO GET IT UNDER CONTROL. BUT THEY DIDN'T *TRUST* US TO.
SO THEY DROPPED IT ON US. THE BOMB.
KKRSH
I SAW THEIR FLESH TURN TO ASH AND THEIR BONES FALL. HUNDREDS OF HEARTBEATS STOPPED. THEY JUDGED US ALL.
AND IN A FLASH OF MAGICAL *LIGHTNING,* I WOKE UP ON A BETTER WORLD--
THIS WORLD DOESN'T NEED ME.
I DON'T BELONG HERE.
SUPERMAN?
THOOOMMM

CHOOOMMMM
FWOOOSHHH
WHAT DO WE DO?
STOP HIM.

THERE'S NOTHING BUT LOSS.
I'VE INCREASED HIS WEIGHT A HUNDREDFOLD.
NOW THERE'S NO NEED TO GET MAD, SUPERMAN. EVEN IF WE'RE FROM DIFFERENT PLACES--
--WE'RE STILL FRIENDS.
ZZZZZZ
THOOMM
I'M TIRED OF LOSS.

I'M NOT MAD, STARMAN.
I'M SORRY.
MY GRAVITY POWERS!
K'RAAA-ACH
HE BEAT THEM!
WHAT DID YOU SAY TO HIM, TODD?
NOTHING...
BOOOOMMM

I SEE HIM, ALAN. HEADING UP SEVENTH.
SONNUVAGUN IS FAST. MAYBE AS FAST AS WALLY.
WHERE THE HECK DID HE GO--?
IT'S TIME TO GIVE UP.
GOOD--
--BYE...
TRIX
LOOK!
UP IN THE--
FWWOOOOSH
NDOM HOUSE
IS THAT...?

POPE
IS THAT SUPERMAN?
GIVING UP NEVER HELPED ANYONE, MISS.
TRUST ME ON THAT.

THE BATCAVE.
...APPEARING THIS AFTERNOON AFTER A 15-YEAR-OLD LEAPT FROM THE TOP OF...
...ORIGINALLY THOUGHT TO BE SUPERMAN, THERE'VE BEEN SOME CONFLICTING REPORTS AS TO WHO THIS "MAN OF STEEL" REALLY...
...CAN SIMPLY ASK, IS THERE ANOTHER SUPERMAN FLYING THROUGH THE SKIES? AND IF SO...
WHY?
CENTRAL CITY.
THE FLASH MUSEUM.
HERE IT IS, JAY.
BARRY WAS ALWAYS BETTER AT NAVIGATING THROUGH TIME AND SPACE THAN I WAS.
WELL, YEAH, JAY. HE BUILT THE COSMIC TREADMILL.
FLASH! HELP ME!
I'M COMING!
I'M COMING!
...hnnfff...
...HELP...
HOW IS SHE?
HER PARENTS ARE FLYING IN TO MEET HER AT THE HOSPITAL.
WE'LL MAKE SURE SHE GETS THE HELP--
I MEAN POWER GIRL.
WHEN THEY STARTED CALLING ME SUPERMAN--
"-- SHE FLEW AWAY."

NEVER BEEN COMFORTABLE WITH TIME TRAVEL.
I'M NOT TALKING ABOUT TIME TRAVEL, WALLY.
I'M TALKING ABOUT ALTERING OUR VIBRATIONAL FREQUENCIES.
ATIVE
I'M TALKING ABOUT TRAVELING TO A *PARALLEL* EARTH.
YOU THINK YOU ARE A *GOD*, CHROMA?
BWAASH
AAAIIEEEE!!
Um, EXCUSE ME, GREEN LANTERN...
GRANDMA'S COOKING UP SOME FOOD FOR EVERYONE AND SHE WANTED ME TO LET YOU KNOW THAT, *uh*...
...THEY'RE HERE.
YOU WERE A *PRETENDER*, CHROMA.
YOU WERE *NOT* A *GOD*.
I AM A *GOD*.

JUSTICE SOCIETY OF AMERICA #11 cover A by ALEX ROSS

JUSTICE SOCIETY OF AMERICA #11 cover B by DALE EAGLESHAM & DREW GERACI Interior art by EAGLESHAM, RUY JOSÉ & GERACI

FASTER.
THE SECOND COMING

KEYSTONE CITY.

THE FLASH MUSEUM.

I'M JUST MAKING SURE YOU CAN KEEP UP, JAY.

WITH THE SPEED FORCE BACK, IT'S NOT A PROBLEM.

BUT "THANKS" FOR TAKING IT EASY ON THE OLD MAN.

FEELS LIKE WE JUST BROKE THE LIGHT BARRIER, BUT EVERYTHING'S... RED.

THAT'S BECAUSE IT'S NOT THE LIGHT BARRIER, WALLY. IT'S SOME KIND OF UNIVERSE BARRIER.

BUT THE MULTIVERSE WAS DESTROYED A LONG TIME AGO, WASN'T IT? ERASED FROM REALITY AND OUR MINDS LIKE IT NEVER EVEN EXISTED.

THE COSMIC TREADMILL IS SHIFTING OUR VIBRATIONAL FREQUENCIES DOWN. TRYING TO MATCH IT UP WITH A PARALLEL EARTH.

WHICH IS WHY, WHEN THIS OTHER SUPERMAN SHOWED UP CLAIMING TO BE FROM A PARALLEL EARTH--

--I WANTED US TO PULL THE COSMIC TREADMILL OUT OF THE MOTHBALLS.

I SEE SOMETHING, BUT I'M NOT SURE WHAT--

WHOA!
JAY?!
THE TREADMILL'S OLD READINGS SAY WE'RE MATCHED UP WITH UNIVERSE-2--
--BUT THERE'S NOTHING OUT HERE. AND THE TREADMILL'S BREAKING APART.
I'M POWERING IT DOWN. WE'LL SHIFT BACK TO--
BLAM
WE'RE BACK IN THE MUSEUM.
I'M NOT SURE WHERE WE JUST WENT OR WHAT WE JUST SAW--
--BUT SOMETHING'S OUT THERE, JAY.

THE FLASH
Jay Garrick.
The original Fastest Man Alive.
MR. TERRIFIC
Michael Holt.
Third smartest man in the world.
DR. MID-NITE
Dr. Pieter Cross.
Super-hero surgeon.
GREEN LANTERN
Alan Scott.
Keeper of the Green Flame.
"SOMETHING ELSE."
HE'S NOT LYING.
BATTERY PARK, NEW YORK.
HEADQUARTERS OF THE JUSTICE SOCIETY OF AMERICA.
HAWKMAN
Carter Hall.
Winged warrior.
STARMAN
Thom Kallor. Unbalanced cosmic cowboy from the future.
STARGIRL
Courtney Whitmore.
Star-powered teenager.
DAMAGE
Grant Emerson.
Human bomb.

WILDCAT
Ted Grant.
Former heavyweight champion.
WILDCAT
Tommy Bronson.
Ted Grant's feral son.
LIBERTY BELLE
Jesse Chambers.
All-American powerhouse.
HOURMAN
Rick Tyler.
Super-strength an hour at a time.
CYCLONE
Maxine Hunkel.
Teenaged wind witch.
MA HUNKEL
Curator of the
JSA brownstone.
CITIZEN STEEL
Nate Heywood.
Indestructible man.
POWER GIRL
Kara Zor-L. Kryptonian survivor
from a parallel universe.

OUR RINGS ARE CONFIRMING HIS DNA IDENTIFICATION.
THEY SAY HE'S KRYPTONIAN.
IF HE'S NOT SUPERMAN, HE'S FOOLING WONDER WOMAN'S LASSO OF TRUTH AND OUR POWER RINGS.
CELLULAR ANALYSIS COMPLETE. 100% MATCH.
CELLULAR ANALYSIS COMPLETE. 100% MATCH.
HE'S SUPERMAN.
ANALYZING HIM WITH YOUR MICROSCOPIC VISION?
I DON'T NEED TO, ALAN. I BELIEVE HIM.
I APPRECIATE THAT.
I KNEW THE BOY SCOUTS WOULD GET ALONG. DIDN'T YOU?!
I DIDN'T WANT TO ASSUME, STARMAN.
THE LAST TIME A GRAY-HAIRED SUPERMAN FROM ANOTHER EARTH SHOWED UP, HE WAS CONDEMNING US FOR ALL THE "MISTAKES" WE MADE.
AND THE JUSTICE SOCIETY IS HERE TO HELP EVERYONE LEARN FROM THOSE MISTAKES, CORRECT?
IT'S LIKE OUR SUPES SAYS, "THE WORLD NEEDS BETTER GOOD GUYS."
ONE SUPERMAN DAMNS US.
THE OTHER BLESSES US.
AND YOU'RE HERE TO MAKE SURE YOUR SON BECOMES ONE OF THEM? YOU CHOSE TO BE A FATHER, TED?
WELL... I GUESS.
THE TED GRANT I KNEW DIDN'T, AND THEN... YOU'RE LUCKY TO HAVE HIM, TOMMY.
WELL... I GUESS.
IT'S LIKE A "SECOND COMING."

LET'S RECONSIDER FLOURISHING THIS EVENT WITH ANY RELIGIOUS IMPLICATIONS, MID-NITE.
WE SHOULD TAKE EVERYTHING INTO CONSIDERATION, MR. TERRIFIC, WOULDN'T YOU AGREE?
RESPECT THEIR BELIEFS AND THEY'LL RESPECT YOURS.

SO THE QUESTION OF THE DAY IS...
...WHAT'S NEXT?
THAT'S *EASY* TO ANSWER, BLACK CANARY.

WHAT'S NEXT IS WE HELP THIS SUPERMAN GET BACK *HOME*.

ANY IDEAS ON HOW WE DO THAT, BATMAN?
BREACHING THE BARRIERS BETWEEN TIME AND SPACE ISN'T EASY, BUT THE LEAGUE'S DONE IT ENOUGH. FROM THE DIMENSION MR. MXYZPTLK CALLS HOME TO ANCIENT ATLANTIS.
STARMAN CREATED A BLACK HOLE THAT APPARENTLY ACTED AS A WORMHOLE INTO A PARALLEL UNIVERSE.
I SUPPOSE I COULD GIVE IT ANOTHER GO, BATMAN! IT WAS JUST, WELL, IT WAS VERY HARD.
AND LOCATING THE RIGHT EARTH AND THE RIGHT TIME. I'D NEED A MAP OF THE MULTIVERSE FOR SOMETHING LIKE THAT!
ANYONE HAVE ONE?!
IS HE--?
STARMAN'S FINE.
INTERESTING DEFINITION OF "FINE."
WE'RE ASSUMING SUPERMAN WANTS TO GO BACK.
IF HIS WORLD NEEDS HELP, I SUGGEST WE ALL FIND A WAY.
THANKS FOR THE THOUGHT, BUT WE CAN'T GO BACK.
WE CAN TRY.
WHEN THE BLACKNESS PULLED ME AWAY, THE EXPLOSIONS WERE TEN TIMES WHAT DESTROYED KANSAS. I WATCHED MY ADOPTED PLANET DIE.
I WATCHED MY HOME DIE. FOR A SECOND TIME.
MY EARTH IS GONE.

"JUST LIKE POWER GIRL'S."

HERE LIES KAL-L

IT'S NOT FAIR.

"IF YOU'RE TRAPPED ON OUR EARTH--"
--WHAT DO WE DO FROM HERE?
"I DON'T KNOW."
...WELCOME TO STAY AT THE BROWNSTONE FOR AS LONG AS YOU WANT.
UNTIL WE FIGURE OUT--
UNTIL YOU FIGURE OUT--
"--WHAT YOU WANT TO DO."
LOOK! DO YOU SEE THEM?!
GET THE CAMERA, ALEX!
THERE AREN'T ANY SCREAMS OF FEAR WHEN THEY LOOK IN THE SKY.
NO ONE RUNS IN A PANIC.

NOT HERE.
DRINK Soder Cola
Big Apple Eatery
THE NEW BROADWAY MUSICAL BATS
...um, I SAW ALL THOSE HOLES IN YOUR COSTUME AND YOU SAID YOU DIDN'T KNOW WHAT YOU WERE GOING TO DO, SO I THOUGHT YOU HAD TO GET SICK OF WEARING THAT ROBE AND, I...
MAXINE'S A THEATER MAJOR.
SHE MADE THIS FOR YOU.
YEAH...
"...JUST IN CASE."
...MULTIPLE EXPLOSIONS ON ELLIS ISLAND...
...COUNTLESS INJURED...
‹...YOU CANNOT LEAVE OUR FAMILY, SONIA...›
...READ YOU, MICHAEL. WHAT DO YOU GOT?
SAT IMAGES MATCHED HER FACE TO ONE OF THE JUSTICE SOCIETY'S NEW LEGACY FILES.
‹YOU BELONG TO US.›
HER NAME IS SONIA SATO.

"SHE USES THE NAME
JUDOMASTER."
"WHO'S WITH HER?"
"THE KETSUEKI-SENSHI--THE BLOOD SOLDIERS. THEY'RE THE KIND OF KILLERS THE YAKUZA PREFERS TO EMPLOY THESE DAYS--
"--ONES WITH SUPER-POWERS.
"SEPPUKU--AN ASSASSIN WHO GAINS IMMORTALITY BY BATHING IN THE BLOOD OF HER VICTIMS.
"KAMIKAZE--A HUMAN BOMB.
"KUNG THE OBAKE--THE SAME ANIMAL SHAPE-SHIFTER WONDER WOMAN'S PLAYED PATTY-CAKE WITH.
"AND SAMURAI--THEIR SUPPOSED POWERHOUSE.

KKKRTCHH
"SONIA SATO'S FATHER WAS YOSHIO SATO--THE LAST AND BEST OF THE TRADITIONAL ASSASSINS THE YAKUZA ONCE EMPLOYED.
"YOSHIO TRIED TO LEAVE THE YAKUZA WHEN HE FOUND OUT HE HAD A DAUGHTER.
"THE BLOOD SOLDIERS KILLED HIM FOR IT."

"ANY RELATION TO SERGEANT HADLEY "RIP" JAGGER-- THE FIRST JUDOMASTER?"
"NONE. SAVE THAT JAGGER'S OLD PROTEGE, TIGER, IS THE LEADER OF THE BLOOD SOLDIERS.
"TIGER'S BEHIND OVER SEVENTY-TWO ASSASSINATIONS IN JAPAN THIS YEAR ALONE.
"JUDOMASTER'S BEEN ON THE RUN FOR GOOD REASON."
A MONTH AGO, JUDOMASTER WENT TO ORACLE FOR HELP--BUT SHE TOOK OFF BEFORE ORACLE HAD A CHANCE TO OFFER HER A CUP OF COFFEE.
WELL, SHE'S HERE NOW, MICHAEL. AND WE'VE GOT HUNDREDS OF PEOPLE IN HARM'S WAY BECAUSE OF IT.
SHE HARDLY SPEAKS A WORD OF ENGLISH.
"THERE'S ONE MORE THING TO BE AWARE OF, ALAN. NO ONE'S SURE HOW SHE DOES IT, BUT THIS NEW JUDOMASTER HAS A UNIQUE ABILITY."
RROOORRR!
<YOU HAVE A SIMPLE CHOICE, SONIA. JOIN US OR YOUR FLESH BECOMES THE OBAKE'S NEXT MEAL.>
<AND YOUR BLOOD MY NEXT BATH.>
RRRRAAAAOO!
"SHE CAN'T BE HIT."

"NOT BY A FIST OR A FOOT.
"A SWORD OR EVEN BULLETS."
"TED WOULD FIND THAT HARD TO BELIEVE, MICHAEL."

‹YOU HAVE MADE YOUR DEFIANCE CLEAR, SONIA.›
‹YOU HAVE NO INTENTION OF SALVAGING WHAT IS LEFT OF YOUR FATHER'S HONOR.›
KRRNCHH
"SOMEHOW, SHE PROJECTS A FIELD THAT THROWS EVERYONE'S AIM OFF."

YOU AND HOURMAN HELP THESE PEOPLE GET CLEAR, DAMAGE. STEEL AND I WILL HEAD--
THAT ONE DUDE'S GLOWING, JESSE. JUST LIKE ME.

"THE ONLY THING JUDOMASTER CAN'T AVOID--"
‹BANZAI.›
BOOOMM
"--IS AN ATTACK THAT'S NOT FOCUSED DIRECTLY AT HER."

THAT BIG FAT GUY JUST BLEW HIMSELF UP! I MEAN, HIS GUTS JUST SPLATTERED ALL OVER THE PLACE.
I HOPE NO KIDS SAW THAT.
HEY, HON-- AM I SEEING THAT RIGHT--?
--OR DID I DRINK ONE TOO MANY MARTINIS AT YOUR MOTHER'S LAST NIGHT?
‹TIGER SAYS YOU BECAME JUDOMASTER TO "REPENT" FOR YOUR FATHER'S LIFE.›
‹TO DESTROY ALL OF YAKUZA.›
‹ONLY A FOOL WOULD DECLARE SUCH A THING.›
‹AND WHAT TYPE OF FOOL ARE YOU?›

‹LISTEN CLOSELY, FRIEND.›
‹I SAW YOU DO YOUR LITTLE MAGIC TRICK. YOU DETONATE YOUR BODY AND RE-FORM. IT'S REAL CUTE.›
NNGG.
‹DO IT AGAIN AND I'LL THROW A FEW NICE PIECES ACROSS THE ATLANTIC.›
‹DO YOU THINK YOU CAN BRING YOURSELF TOGETHER IF YOU'RE AN OCEAN'S LENGTH APART?›
‹I CAN TRY. BANZ--›
KRRAKK
SHE DOESN'T SHOW ANY EMOTION.
SHE DOESN'T SAY A WORD.
NOT A WORD.

THE SOCIETY HELPS WITH THE EVACUATION AND THE CLEANUP LIKE I EXPECT THEM TO.

THOSE THAT ATTACKED JUDOMASTER ARE CARTED AWAY, AND JUDOMASTER HERSELF...

JAPANESE IS ONE OF THE HUNDREDS OF LANGUAGES HAWKMAN SPEAKS FLUENTLY... YET SHE STILL SAYS NOTHING.

THE AUTHORITIES WANT TO ARREST HER.

SO WOULD I.

THIS ISN'T RIGHT!

HEY, WATCH IT--

$@%@ YOU!

GRANT.

SORRY. I JUST WANTED TO SAY SOMETHING--

WE HAVE ENOUGH PEOPLE SAYING SOMETHING, KID--

DAMAGE IS A MEMBER OF THE JUSTICE SOCIETY. HE HAS A RIGHT TO SPEAK HIS MIND--

--AS LONG AS HE WATCHES HIS LANGUAGE.

I...I ONLY WANTED TO SAY...I HAD A PROBLEM IN ATLANTA WHEN I LOST CONTROL, AND...IT WAS WAY WORSE THAN THIS...WAY WORSE. NO ONE WAS THERE TO...

...LOOK, JUST BECAUSE THERE'S A CRACK IN SOMETHING DOESN'T MEAN YOU THROW IT AWAY.

WHAT? WHAT THE HELL DOES THAT MEAN?

THAT'S OUR BOY.
IT'S A DIFFERENT WORLD.

POWER GIRL?

I'M SORRY.
I DIDN'T MEAN TO STARTLE YOU.
YOU... DIDN'T.
I UNDERSTAND IF MY BEING HERE UPSETS YOU.

IT'S JUST--IT'S STRANGE. YOU EVEN LOOK...
YOU LOOK JUST LIKE HIM, TO BE HONEST. YOU SOUND LIKE HIM.
AND YOU LOOK AND SOUND LIKE *MY* COUSIN.

LOSING THINGS, YOU CAN GIVE UP SOMETIMES. YOU CAN GET THAT URGE TO JUST WALK AWAY FROM IT ALL.
YOU ***NEVER*** WALKED AWAY. YOU ***NEVER*** GAVE UP.
I DIDN'T HAVE A CHOICE.
YES. YES, YOU DID. MY WIFE, LOIS, WAS MURDERED BY THE JOKER.
I DIDN'T KNOW--

IN RETALIATION, THE JOKER WAS KILLED BY A METAHUMAN NAMED MAGOG.
MAGOG WAS ACQUITTED, MOSTLY DUE TO PUBLIC SUPPORT. THEY ***APPROVED*** OF HOW HE DEALT WITH THAT MANIAC.
I WALKED AWAY FROM IT ALL AFTER THAT.

YOU WERE THE FIRST NEW RECRUIT THE FOUNDERS BROUGHT INTO THE JUSTICE SOCIETY. YOU EXCEEDED ALL THEIR EXPECTATIONS.
YOU FOUND A NEW HOME AND A NEW PURPOSE.
MAYBE I CAN TOO.
WE MIGHT NOT BE FAMILY LIKE YOU AND YOUR COUSIN WERE, KAREN...
...BUT I HOPE WE CAN LEARN TO BE.

MISSING GIRL FROM
MARSHFIELD, WISCONSIN.
KEPT HER. AND BACK UP. THEY SAID HE MIGHT NOT WALK AGAIN.
HER KIDNAPPER HAD BRUTALIZED HER IN UNIMAGINABLE WAYS OVER THE SIX DAYS HE HELD HER. HE DID THINGS SHE'LL NEVER RECOVER FROM.
NEXT TIME I'LL MAKE SURE.
TODAY, THE SCENE IS SOMETHING DIFFERENT. SANITATION WORKERS DISCOVERED THE BODY AT SEVEN THIS MORNING.
SOME SUPERHUMAN THE DEPARTMENT WASN'T VERY FAMILIAR WITH. HE CALLED HIMSELF CHROMA. HE CLAIMED HE WAS A GOD.
WITH THAT UNIFORM, I'M NOT SURE WHAT HE WAS A GOD OF. MAYBE CRAYOLA.
THE F.B.I.'S BEST AND BRIGHTEST FROM QUANTICO HAVE BEEN ON THE SCENE FOR AN HOUR. FIRST, THEY BAGGED AND TAGGED WHAT ENVIRONMENTAL EVIDENCE THEY COULD FIND.
THEN THEY TURNED THEIR ATTENTION TO THE BODY.
ONE MADE THE MISTAKE OF TOUCHING IT.
HIS SKIN AND HAIR TURNED WHITE. HE WENT DEAF AND BLIND.
THAT'S WHEN I GOT THE CALL FROM AGENT JULIE ADAMS. SHE CONTACTS ME WHEN THERE'S A CRIME SCENE THEY CAN'T CRACK. OR WHEN THERE'S A LITTLE EXTRA JUSTICE TO BE HANDED OUT.
THEY USED TO KNOW ME AS SPECIAL AGENT JEFFREY GRAVES. BUT THAT WAS BEFORE DIRECTOR MUELLER LET ME GO BECAUSE I WAS SUPPLYING CASE INFORMATION TO MY EX-PARTNER, TREY THOMPSON.
FBI

TODAY, THEY CALL ME
MR. AMERICA.
AND TODAY, THE HUNT BEGINS.
FBI
FBI
FBI

JUSTICE SOCIETY OF AMERICA #12 cover A by ALEX ROSS

JUSTICE SOCIETY OF AMERICA #12 cover B and interior art by DALE EAGLESHAM & RUY JOSÉ

BATTERY PARK, NEW YORK.
HEADQUARTERS OF THE JUSTICE SOCIETY OF AMERICA.
HELLO?
I DON'T SEE A "WELCOME HOME" BANNER, THUNDERBOLT.
I CAN CONJURE ONE UP IF IT'D MAKE YOU FEEL BETTER. JUST GOTTA MAKE A WISH, JAKEEM.
I DON'T SEE ANY PICTURES OF US ANYWHERE EITHER.
WELL, HANGING PICTURES IS THE LAST THING YOU DO WHEN YOU MOVE IN.
I THINK I LIKED THE OLD BROWNSTONE BETTER.
Eh. ME TOO.
KEYSTONE
BIALYA
I AIN'T DOIN' THIS FOR YOUR ENTERTAINMENT.
WEREN'T YOU TELLING ME TO STOP WHINING AND FIGHT, POP?
THAT FIGHT WAS FER CHARITY, NOT LAUGHS. THIS IS A SERIOUS EXPERIMENT HERE.
NO ONE'S LAUGHING, POP. YET.
HEY.

Alan Scott.
Keeper of the Green Flame.
Jay Garrick.
The original Fastest Man Alive.
Carter Hall.
Winged warrior.
Kara Zor-L. Kryptonian survivor
from a parallel universe.
Kal-El.
The Man of Steel from Earth-22.
WHO THE $%#@ ARE YOU?!
YEAH! WHO THE $%#@ ARE YOU?!
PASS THE-- OOOPS.
JAKEEM THUNDER
STARGIRL
CYCLONE
WILDCAT
WILDCAT
Jakeem Williams. Keeper of the
Courtney Whitmore.
Star-powered teenager
Maxine Hunkel.
Teenaged wind witch
Ted Grant.
Former heavyweight champion
Tommy Bronson.
Ted Grant's feral son

Michael Holt. Third-smartest man in the world.
Dr. Pieter Cross. Super-hero surgeon.
Jesse Chambers. All-American powerhouse.
Rick Tyler. Super-strength an hour at a time.
WHERE'D I GET THE POPCORN? I GET IT WHERE I ALWAYS GET IT, NATE. THE MOVIE THEATRE SEVEN BLOCKS NORTH AND TWO BLOCKS WEST!
YOU KNOW WE HAVE SOME IN THE KITCHEN. YOU JUST HAVE TO PUT IT IN THE MICROWAVE.
PUT IT IN THE MICROWAVE? OH, NO. I COULDN'T BE THAT CRUEL.
NEW
DAMAGE
STARMAN
CITIZEN STEEL
JUDOMASTER
Grant Emerson. Human bomb.
Thom Kallor. Unbalanced cosmic cowboy from the future.
Nate Heywood. Indestructible man
Sonia Sato.

WELL, I'LL BE DAMNED. LOOK WHO FINALLY GRACES THE EVER-EXPANDING J.S. OF A. WITH THEIR PRESENCE.
HOW YA DOIN', KID? JOHNNY?
S'UP, WILDCAT. WHAT'S WITH ALL THE NEW--?
OH! IT'S A PLEASURE AND A PLEASURE TO MEET YOU BOTH. YOU'RE THE BOY AND HIS WONDERFUL, WACKY GENIE!
WELL, HE'S FRIENDLY. HOW YA DO?
I'M STARMAN.
I'M FROM THE FUTURE.
WEEEOOOEEEE!
I'M TOMMY BRONSON. WILDCAT'S KID.
WILDCAT'S KID IS A WEREWOLF?
HE'S TED'S KID?!
WERE-PANTHER ACTUALLY. WELL, FROM WHAT DR. MID-NITE'S HYPOTHESIZED.
YOU'RE NOT ATOM SMASHER.
DAMAGE.
THAT'S A NEW COSTUME, huh? YOU EVEN GOT A MASK LIKE YOUR DAD! YOU GONNA CALL YOURSELF THE ATOM?!
...NO.
ATOM BOMB?
NO.
WHAT ABOUT ATOM SMASHER TWO?
DAMAGE.
DAMAGE IS COOL.
AND YOU! AT YOUR SERVICE, COMMANDER STEEL!
NATE'S A COMMANDER?! ATTEN-HUUTT!
DON'T SALUTE. MY GRANDFATHER WAS THE MILITARY MAN, NOT ME.
THE PAPERS CALL ME CITIZEN STEEL.
YOU DO KNOW THE FLOOR'S CRACKING UNDER YOUR FEET.
I'VE GOT A BIT OF A WEIGHT PROBLEM.

WHO'S THE ASIAN *HOTTIE?*
NEWEST KID ON THE BLOCK-- *JUDOMASTER.* SHE WAS INVOLVED IN A BRAWL ON ELLIS ISLAND YESTERDAY.
LEFT A LOT OF PEOPLE IN THE HOSPITAL BECAUSE SHE WAS *CARELESS* CRACKIN' SKULLS.
DAMAGE TALKED THE COPS OUT OF *ARRESTING* HER. SO SHE'S IN OUR CUSTODY UNTIL HER COURT DATE.
I THINK SOMEONE HAS A *CRUSH.* LIKE COLOSSAL BOY AND YERA! DREAM *DATES!*
KNOCK IT *OFF,* STARMAN!
YO, WHY'S SHE IN THE RING WEARIN' GLOVES?
MR. TERRIFIC SAID SHE'S ONE OF THE BEST FIGHTERS IN THE WORLD.
TERRIFIC *DOESN'T* KNOW EVERYTHING.
SHE'S SUPPOSED TO BE *UNTOUCHABLE.*
UNTOUCHABLE?
EVERYONE'S SAYING SHE PROJECTS SOME KIND OF FIELD THAT THROWS HER ATTACKER'S AIM OFF. THEY SAY SHE CAN'T BE *HIT.*
BUT YOUR *DAD* IS GONNA *TRY, huh?* DAMN, I *GOTTA* SEE THIS.
WE *ALL* DO.
I TOLD YOU, TOMMY, THIS AIN'T *DINNER THEATER,* IT'S *IMPORTANT* RESEARCH--
-- DON'T FIGHT WATCH
JAPANESE HAWKMAN.
DOESN'T WILDCAT?
JUDOMASTER FIGHT ?
DO YOU UNDERSTAND ME?
SLOWER DOESN'T *HELP,* WEBSTER.
WELL, HOW YOU GONNA TELL HER WHAT TO DO IN THE *RING?*

UNIVERSAL LANGUAGE, JAKEEM.

DING-A-LING LING!

LET'S SEE IF YOU CAN HIT THE TARGET, POP.

DINGG

YEAH, YEAH.

UFFF!

"DID YOU EVER THINK DAMAGE WOULD STEP UP TO THE PLATE LIKE THAT?"

"WE OWE HIS ATTITUDE ADJUSTMENT TO LIBERTY BELLE AND HOURMAN, ALAN. STARMAN'S IMPROVING. CYCLONE'S LEARNED HOW TO BREATHE BETWEEN SENTENCES."
"THEY'RE NOT ROOKIES ANYMORE."
"SO WE'RE ALL IN AGREEMENT THEN?"

WHO'S NEXT?
THERE'S ONE CANDIDATE WE'VE BEEN REQUESTED TO MEET, WHICH MR. TERRIFIC AND THE GIRLS ARE HANDLING.
AND THERE ARE MORE THAN A HANDFUL OF LEGACIES, DIRECT AND INDIRECT, THAT WE'VE PUT ON A SHORT LIST.
BUT THIS ONE. THIS ONE COMES FROM A DIFFERENT LEGACY.
IS THAT TRUE?
SANDY CONFIRMED IT THIS MORNING.
THEN I SUGGEST WE HANDLE HIM PERSONALLY.

NEW ORLEANS.
H CLINIC
"HIS NAME IS MARKUS CLAY."
BLAMM
TINKK
"AMAZING-MAN."

I DON'T RECOGNIZE HIM.
IF THERE WAS AN AMAZING-MAN ON MY EARTH, I NEVER MET HIM.
THERE'S BEEN MOR THAN ONE HERE.
"BACK IN THE '40s, NEARLY EVERY AFRICAN-AMERICAN MYSTERY-MAN KEPT TO THE SHADOWS.
"IT WASN'T UNTIL MARKUS CLAY'S GRANDFATHER, WILL EVERETT, THAT SOMEONE STEPPED INTO THE SPOTLIGHT.
"EVERETT WAS THE FIRST AMAZING-MAN.
"HE COULD TRANSFORM HIMSELF INTO WHATEVER HE TOUCHED. AN ABILITY HE PASSED DOWN TO HIS GRANDSONS.
"AFTER THE WAR, AMAZING-MAN'S IDENTITY WAS REVEALED TO THE WORLD BY J. EDGAR HOOVER. THANKS TO HOOVER, WILL EVERETT AND HIS FAMILY RECEIVED DEATH THREATS CONSTANTLY.
"IN THE EARLY '60s, EVERETT'S NEPHEW, A CIVIL RIGHTS WORKER, AND TWO OF HIS FRIENDS DISAPPEARED IN MISSISSIPPI.
"AMAZING-MAN PULLED THEIR CAR OUT OF THE SWAMP. HE FOUND THEIR BODIES IN THE TRUNK.
"AFTER THAT, AMAZING-MAN MOVED HIS ATTENTION AWAY FROM THE EXTRAORDINARY AND ONTO EVERYDAY AMERICAN LIFE.
"HE LED MARCHES AGAINST SEGREGATION ACROSS THE COUNTRY. QUELLED RACE RIOTS IN DETROIT. AND HE WAS THE ONE THAT HUNTED DOWN AND CAPTURED MARTIN LUTHER KING, JR.'S KILLER--JAMES EARL RAY.
EQUAL RIGHTS NOW!
WE DEMAND
"ALONG WITH KING AND MALCOLM X, AMAZING-MAN IS ONE OF THE MOST IMPORTAN HISTORICAL FIGURES IN AMERICAN CIVIL RIGHTS."

"WILL EVERETT'S FIRST GRANDSON TOOK ON THE AMAZING-MAN IDENTITY A FEW YEARS AGO, BUT HE DIED FIGHTING THE MIST.
MY GRANDFATHER SAID, "THOSE LOST IN HATE AND DESPAIR CAN FIND AMAZING TRANSFORMATION."
"AFTER HURRICANE KATRINA, MARKUS CLAY CAME ON THE SCENE. AND HE'S BEEN MAKING QUITE A NAME FOR HIMSELF."
THIS BOY'S HOME WAS WIPED AWAY. HE AND HIS FAMILY WERE TRAPPED WITH NOWHERE TO GO. HIS GRANDMOTHER DIED BECAUSE SHE DIDN'T HAVE HER MEDICATION.
NOT
HE SAYS THEY FORGOT ABOUT US. THEY TURNED AWAY WHEN WE NEEDED HELP.
BUT HE USES THEIR MISTAKES TO JUSTIFY MURDERING AND ROBBING HIS NEIGHBOR.
NOTHING JUSTIFIES THAT.
WE NEED TO STOP BLAMING AND START TAKING RESPONSIBILITY FOR THE HERE AND NOW.
WE NEED TO LEARN TO SWIM IN THE WATERS THAT STILL HAUNT THIS CITY.
WE NEED TO FIND THAT AMAZING TRANSFORMATION WITHIN EACH ONE OF US.
9TH WARD
AMAZING-MAN.
POWER GIRL. AND... SUPERMAN.
HAWKMAN TOLD ME YOU WERE COMING. I'M HAPPY TO DISCUSS MY POTENTIAL INVOLVEMENT WITH THE JUSTICE SOCIETY--
--BUT FIRST, SINCE YOU'RE DOWN HERE, I COULD USE SOME HELP.

BEFORE KATRINA, THIS THING WAS OUT IN THE GULF.
HOW DID IT GET HERE?
IT FOUND ITS WAY THROUGH THE LEVEE FLOODWALLS, SMASHED THROUGH THE NEIGHBORHOOD AND LANDED HERE WHEN THE WATER RECEDED.
THIS BARGE IS MORE THAN A MORBID PHOTO OP.
IT'S A SYMBOL OF THE MANY FAILURES THAT NEARLY DESTROYED THIS CITY.
I WANT IT THE HELL OUT.
TNC 4727

MY NAME IS JEFFREY GRAVES.
FORMER AGENT WITH THE F.B.I. SPECIALIZING IN PROFILING AND CRIMINAL SCIENCE, I NOW GO BY THE CODE NAME: MR. AMERICA.
LAST NIGHT, I CAUGHT A CHILD KILLER IN TACOMA. TONIGHT, I TURN BACK TO THE BIZARRE CASE THE NEWSPAPERS ARE CALLING "THE HEARTBREAK SLAYER."
JESUS.
TWO METAHUMAN CRIMINALS POSING AS DEMIGODS HAVE BEEN FOUND WITH HOLES BLOWN THROUGH THEIR CHESTS.
TONIGHT, A THIRD VICTIM TURNED UP OUTSIDE OF MANHATTAN. A GUY WITH WINGS WHO WENT BY THE NAME PROTEUS.
PROTEUS WAS A MEMBER OF A SUPERHUMAN TERRORIST GANG CALLED THE NEW OLYMPIANS. MY FORMER PARTNER, AGENT JULIE ADAMS, GAVE ME THE LOCATIONS THEY'VE BEEN KNOWN TO OPERATE OUT OF.
THE SECOND ONE I VISIT IS A PSEUDO-GREEK TEMPLE HIDDEN UNDER THE NEW YORK SUBWAY.
PROTEUS' TEAMMATES AREN'T IN ANY CONDITION TO BE INTERROGATED.
ARGUS.
ANTAEUS.
VULCANUS.
DIANA.
NOX.
FIVE MORE VICTIMS. EACH ONE POSING AS A DEMIGOD.
AND THEY HAVEN'T BEEN DEAD FOR MORE THAN A FEW--
EACH ONE WITH A HOLE BLOWN THROUGH THEIR CHEST.

CHICAGO.
WE MADE A DEAL WITH ANISSA WHEN SHE WAS TWELVE. SHE PROMISED US SHE WOULDN'T PURSUE THE KIND OF LIFE I DID UNTIL AFTER SHE GRADUATED FROM MED SCHOOL.
WE THOUGHT SHE'D GROW OUT OF WANTING TO WEAR A MASK.
THE NIGHT SHE GRADUATED, SHE BECAME THUNDER.
AND BEFORE WE COULD SAY "NO," SHE WAS A MEMBER OF THE NEW OUTSIDERS.
IT WASN'T THE SAME OUTSIDERS REX AND I WERE ON. BACK THEN, BATMAN RAN A TIGHT SHIP. WE STEPPED OUT OF LINE, HE'D DRAG US BACK INTO FORMATION.
THESE OUTSIDERS PLAYED A LITTLE TOO FAST AND LOOSE FOR US.
THANKFULLY, BATMAN'S BACK.
THANKFULLY.
I DON'T WANT MY YOUNGER DAUGHTER MAKING THE SAME MISTAKES ANISSA HAS, MR. TERRIFIC.
THUNDER'S A WELL-RESPECTED MEMBER OF THE COMMUNITY, JEFF.
HER ROAD THERE COULD'VE BEEN A LOT EASIER.
BUT I HEARD, WELL, EVERYONE SAYS YOU'RE THE NUMBER ONE TEACHER IN THE COUNTRY. LIKE A SUPER-TEACHER WHO SHOOTS LIGHTNING AND--
I DO WHAT I CAN FOR PUBLIC EDUCATION.
DON'T BE SO MODEST, JEFF. YOU HELPED TRANSFORM DECAYING SCHOOL DISTRICTS IN GOTHAM, CHICAGO AND BRICK CITY INTO SOME OF THE FINEST IN THE NATION.
THEN WHY DOES YOUR DAUGHTER NEED THE JUSTICE SOCIETY?

IN THE CLASSROOM, JEFF'S THE MOST WONDERFUL TEACHER YOU COULD EVER *HAVE.* AND HE'S *GREAT* WITH OUR KIDS.
IT'S JUST, WHEN IT COMES TO THEIR *POWERS--*
MUTE
29

KRRZZZZZTTTTT

JENNIFER!

HIS *FUSE* CAN GET A LITTLE *SHORT.*

COMPANY TONIGHT.
HI.
I LIKE YOUR COSTUME.
I DON'T THINK IT'S A COSTUME, CYCLONE.
JENNIFER'S GENERATING SOME KIND OF ELECTRICAL FIELD.
IT TRIGGERS EVERY TIME SHE TOUCHES ANYTHING ELECTRONIC. LASTS FOR FIVE OR TEN MINUTES.
SO THIS APPLE FELL CLOSER TO THE TREE THAN THUNDER.
OH! YOU COULD CALL YOURSELF LIGHTNING. THUNDER AND LIGHTNING!
I'M SURE SHE'S HEARD THAT BEFORE, MAXINE.
ONLY ABOUT A THOUSAND TIMES.
BESIDES, MY SISTER WOULD KILL ME IF I DID THAT. SHE'S ALREADY ÜBER MAD THAT DAD WOULDN'T LET HER USE HER POWERS WHEN SHE WAS MY AGE.
DADS ARE ALWAYS HARDEST ON THE OLDEST. MY BROTHER GETS AWAY WITH EVERYTHING.
I DON'T HAVE ANY BROTHERS OR SISTERS BUT SOMETIMES I THINK THAT'S WHY MY PARENTS WERE SO FOCUSED ON ME WHEN I WAS A KID AND IT WAS LIKE I COULDN'T JUST BE WHO I WANTED TO BE UNTIL I STARTED HANGING OUT WITH MY GRANDMA AND THE JUSTICE SOCIETY AND YOU MIGHT BE THE SAME IF YOU HANG OUT THERE TOO MAYBE WE CAN ALL SLEEP OVER IN THE SAME ROOM TONIGHT AND MAKE NEW COSTUMES!
WHATDOYOUTHINK?
I THINK YOU TALK A LOT.

SORRY, DAD.
YOU TRIED TO USE YOUR CELL PHONE AGAIN, DIDN'T YOU?
KINDA.
JENNIFER.
ROCHELLE WAS SUPPOSED TO PICK ME UP AN HOUR AGO. SHE JUST GOT HER DRIVER'S LICENSE.
ONE-- I DON'T TRUST ANY SIXTEEN-YEAR-OLD WHO DRIVES AN M-CLASS MERCEDES.
AND TWO--

MR. AMERICA BEAT US HERE BY TEN MINUTES.
THERE'S NO CELL RECEPTION FOUR STORIES BENEATH THE "E" LINE.
AND YOU DIDN'T HEAR FROM HIM AFTER THAT, AGENT ADAMS?
ARE YOU INVESTIGATING "THE HEARTBREAK SLAYER"?
NO. I'M RECRUITING.
HEY, HON, TAKE A LOOK AT THIS.
FBI
THIRD DEGREE BURNS COVER A THIRD OF MY BACK. MY THROAT'S BURNING FROM THE SMOKE.
TREY THOMPSON'S LIFE FLASHES BEFORE MY EYES. JOINING THE BUREAU. BECOMING MY PARTNER. LOSING HIS JOB. PUTTING ON THE MR. AMERICA MASK. LOSING HIS FAMILY. AND THEN...
...WHEN I GET TO THE END OF HIS LIFE, HE LOOKS RIGHT AT ME--
WHAT IS IT, RICK?
IT WAS CARVED INTO THE COLUMN.
WHAT'S IT MEAN?
--AND TREY TELLS ME WHERE TO GO.

"I'M SURPRISED YOU'RE ALL SURPRISED."
NORTHERN AFGHANISTAN.
"NOT EVERYONE WITH POWERS WEARS COSTUMES. A LOT OF 'EM WEAR UNIFORMS.
"HECK, LAST I HEARD, THERE WERE OVER THREE HUNDRED OF US SERVING IN THE ARMED FORCES.
BRATTTATATAT
"I'M JUST ONE OF 'EM."
FAZOW
THOOM

LANCE CORPORAL DAVID REID, RIGHT?

YEAH, THOUGH MOST EVERYONE CALLS ME *"LANCE"* 'CAUSE OF ***THIS*** LITTLE ***GADGET***. IT HELPS FOCUS SOME KINDA ENERGY I GOT BUILT UP ***INSIDE*** ME.

I WASN'T AWARE THERE WERE SO MANY SUPERHUMANS ACTIVE IN THE UNITED STATES MILITARY.

BRASS DON'T LIKE ADVERTISING IT. FOR OBVIOUS REASONS.

YOUR SQUAD'S SEEN A LOT OF ACTION THIS WEEK.

NOTHING MORE THAN NORMAL.

YOUR TATTOO IS PULSATING...

IT'S ACTUALLY MORE LIKE A ***BRAND***.

A... BRAND?

I WAS WITH ONE OF THE FIRST PLATOONS THAT WENT INSIDE BAGHDAD. WE WERE ASSIGNED TO HALT THE LOOTING AND VANDALISM THAT HIT THAT MUSEUM...

TRACKED ONE OF THE LOOTERS. FOUND AN ARTIFACT.

I TOUCHED IT. FELT LIKE MY ***BLOOD*** WAS ON FIRE. THEN I BLACKED OUT.

DOCTORS SAY THIS ***EYE*** OPENED UP ON MY ARM.

WOKE UP THREE WEEKS LATER. AND EVERY TIME I ***COUGHED,*** I'D RELEASE THIS PLASMA ENERGY.

Y'KNOW, I HEARD THE JUSTICE SOCIETY WERE OUT THERE RECRUITIN', BUT OUT OF ALL THE OTHERS IN THE MILITARY-- WHY ME?

WE'RE NOT HERE BECAUSE YOU'RE IN THE MILITARY, DAVID.
WE'RE HERE BECAUSE OF WHO YOUR GREAT-GRANDFATHER WAS.

MY GREAT-GRANDFATHER?
MY GREAT-GRANDFATHER WAS FRANKLIN D. ROOSEVELT.
PRESIDENT ROOSEVELT WAS THE MAN WHO BROUGHT THE JUSTICE SOCIETY OF AMERICA TOGETHER IN THE FIRST PLACE.
HE ASKED US TO PROTECT AMERICA WHILE WE WERE AT WAR OVERSEAS.
YOUR GREAT-GRANDFATHER FOUNDED OUR TEAM, DAVID.
THAT MAKES YOU THE JUSTICE SOCIETY'S MOST IMPORTANT LEGACY.

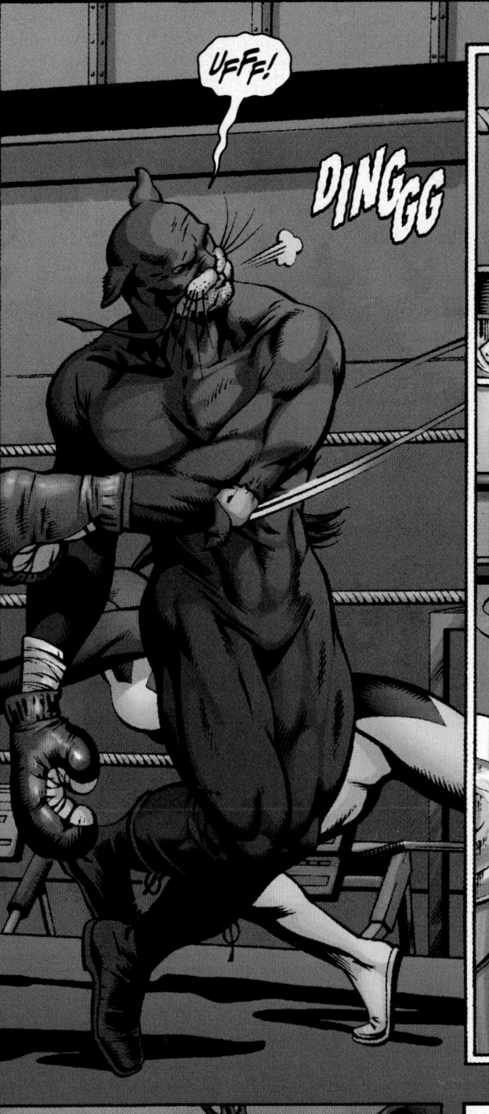
UFFF!
DINGGG

...JUST NEED...
...A SECOND...
THAT'S ROUND *EIGHTEEN,* POP.

SPLAWSH
I TOLD YA, KID. **NO SMOKING** IN THE GYM!

I DON'T THINK SHE WANTS TO DO THIS ANYMORE, WILDCAT.
YOU CAN SEE IT IN HER EYES.
HOW DO YOU KNOW, KID?
GRUUUUUUUSH!
SORRY I DIDN'T... RING THE BUZZER, BUT SOMEONE LEFT THE *FRONT DOOR* OPEN.
OOPS.

ANY OF YOU EVER HEARD OF GOG?
OOO! DÉJÀ VU!
TO BE CONTINUED IN THY KINGDOM COME PART TWO!

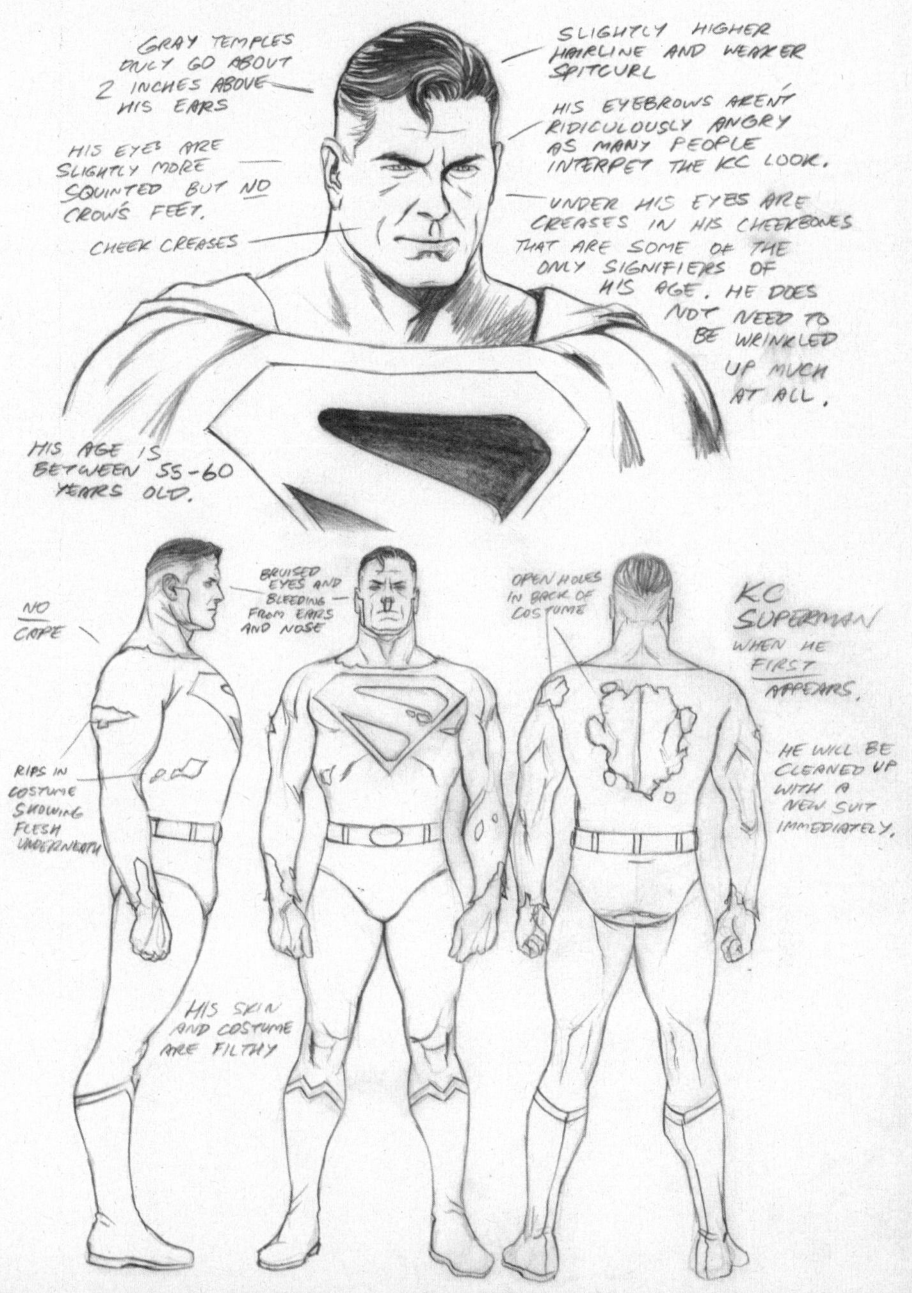
DALE, I THOUGHT I'D USE ONE OF YOUR RECENT SUPERMAN SHOTS TO CLARIFY SOME OF THE DIFFERENCES I SEE TO THE KC SUPERMAN.
GRAY TEMPLES ONLY GO ABOUT 2 INCHES ABOVE HIS EARS
SLIGHTLY HIGHER HAIRLINE AND WEAKER SPITCURL
HIS EYEBROWS AREN'T RIDICULOUSLY ANGRY AS MANY PEOPLE INTERPET THE KC LOOK.
HIS EYES ARE SLIGHTLY MORE SQUINTED BUT NO CROW'S FEET.
UNDER HIS EYES ARE CREASES IN HIS CHEEKBONES THAT ARE SOME OF THE ONLY SIGNIFIERS OF HIS AGE. HE DOES NOT NEED TO BE WRINKLED UP MUCH AT ALL.
CHEEK CREASES
HIS AGE IS BETWEEN 55-60 YEARS OLD.
NO CAPE
BRUISED EYES AND BLEEDING FROM EARS AND NOSE
OPEN HOLES IN BACK OF COSTUME
KC SUPERMAN WHEN HE FIRST APPEARS.
RIPS IN COSTUME SHOWING FLESH UNDERNEATH
HE WILL BE CLEANED UP WITH A NEW SUIT IMMEDIATELY.
HIS SKIN AND COSTUME ARE FILTHY

SKETCHES/CHARACTER DESIGNS

BY ALEX ROSS

COVER #10 SKETCH

COVER #12 SKETCH

MR. AMERICA

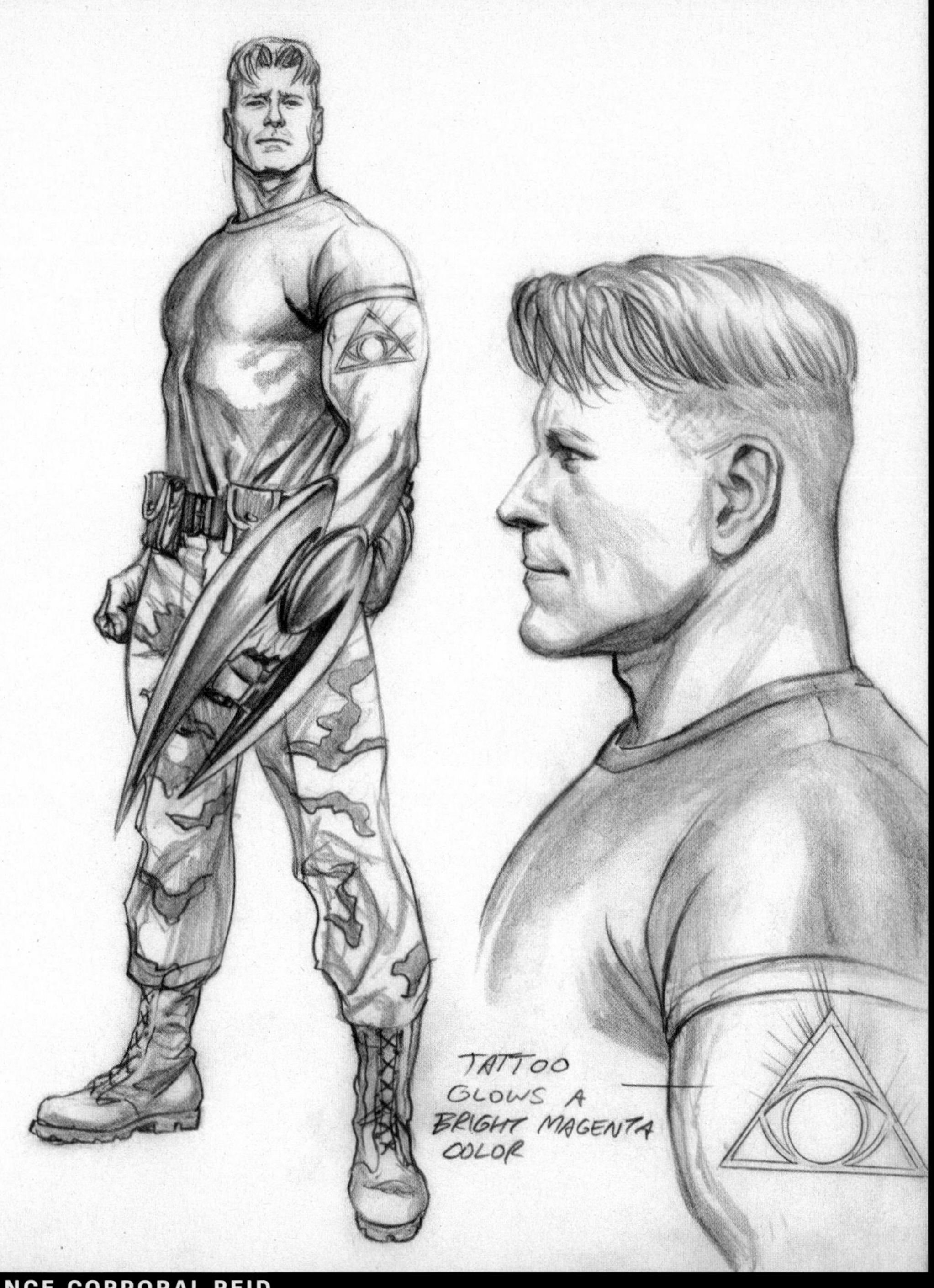

LANCE CORPORAL REID

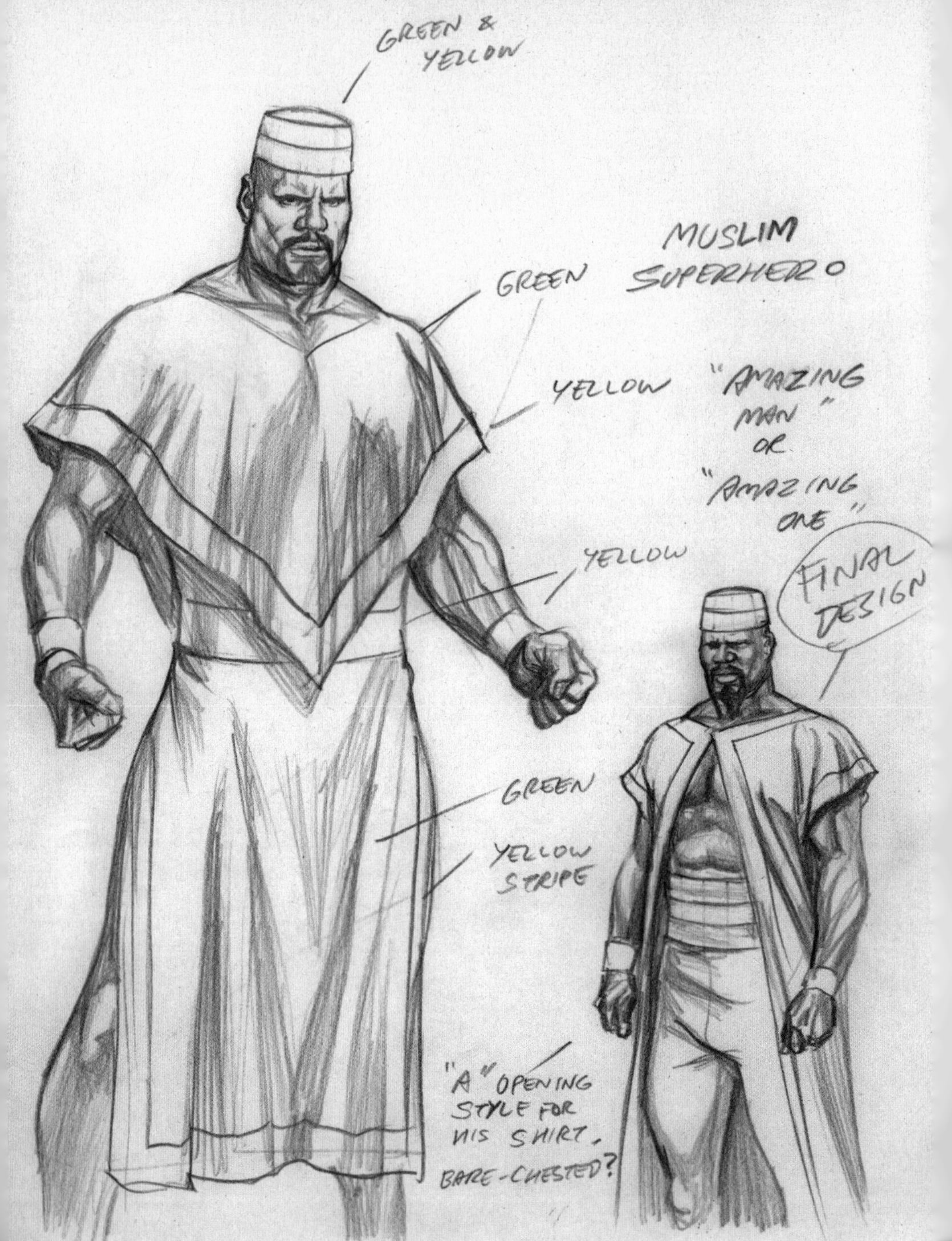
GREEN & YELLOW
MUSLIM SUPERHERO
GREEN
YELLOW
"AMAZING MAN" OR "AMAZING ONE"
YELLOW
FINAL DESIGN
GREEN
YELLOW STRIPE
"A" OPENING STYLE FOR HIS SHIRT. BARE-CHESTED?

AMAZING-MAN

USTICE SOCIETY OF AMERICA #5 & 6 COVERS BY ALEX ROSS

READ MORE ADVENTURES OF AMERICA'S FIRST AND GREATEST SUPER-HERO TEAM IN THESE COLLECTIONS FROM DC COMICS:

THE JUSTICE SOCIETY RETURNS

The members of the JSA must divide into seven teams to save the Earth from the being destroyed by a mad god named Stalker!

James Robinson and **David Goyer** are joined by some of the industry's most respected talents including **Geoff Johns, Mark Waid, Chuck Dixon, Ron Marz, Chris Weston** and **Michael Lark.**

JSA: THE GOLDEN AGE

JAMES ROBINSON
PAUL SMITH

JSA: ALL-STARS

GEOFF JOHNS/JEPH LOEB
TIM SALE/DARWYN COOKE
BARRY KITSON

JSA: JUSTICE BE DONE

JAMES ROBINSON
GEOFF JOHNS

SEARCH THE GRAPHIC NOVELS SECTION OF

www.DCCOMICS.com

FOR ART AND INFORMATION ON ALL OF OUR BOOKS!

"THE EARTH WHERE THE SUPER-HUMAN SOCIETY RAN WILD!"

THANKS FOR GETTING ME OUT OF THAT PAINT FACTORY.
THEY WERE ALL OUT OF THE COLOR YELLOW. DID YOU NOTICE THAT?
YOU... KNOW ME?
OF COURSE I KNOW YOU. I WAS ON MY WAY FROM THE FUTURE TO THE PAST, BUT IT WASN'T SUPPOSED TO BE ME GOING BACK--
--DON'T TELL BRAINY--
--SO I WENT ZIP, ZIP, ZOOM FROM OUR EARTH TO EARTH-22.
I FLEW AROUND WITH YOU AFTER YOU STOPPED AMERICOMMANDO AND THE MINUTEMEN FROM TEARING APART THE STATUE OF LIBERTY... AND EVERYBODY ON IT!
THAT'S WHEN IT GOT BETTER.
YOU WERE THERE, AND YOU--
--AND YOU!
ME?

IS THIS HEAVEN?
MAN, HE DOES LOOK JUST LIKE PEE GEE'S COUSIN.
POWER GIRL'S PARALLEL EARTH WAS DESTROYED A LONG TIME AGO, TED. AND THE SUPERMAN THERE DIED. ALONG WITH THE REST OF THE MULTIVERSE.
MAYBE KAL-L WAS RESURRECTED.
MAYBE HE'S FROM THE FUTURE.
THE FUTURE, WILDCAT?
THAT'S WHERE I COME FROM, NOT HIM.
STARMAN, WE ASKED EVERYONE TO WAIT OUTSIDE.
BUT HE'S MY FRIEND, ALAN.
STOP PUSHING, MAXINE!
STOP PUSHING, GRANDMA!
SUPERMAN'S MY FRIEND FROM ANOTHER EARTH!
52 MINUS 30! SECOND STAR TO THE RIGHT AND STRAIGHT ON UNTIL MORNING!
THAT'S WHAT I ALWAYS SAY.

HAWKMAN
Carter Hall. Winged warrior.
MR. TERRIFIC
Michael Holt. Third smartest man in the world.
DR. MID-NITE
Dr. Pieter Cross. Super-hero surgeon.
WILDCAT
Tommy Bronson. Ted Grant's feral son.
I WATCHED ALL OF YOU DIE.
CITIZEN STEEL
Nate Heywood. Indestructible man.
STARGIRL
Courtney Whitmore. Star-powered teenager.
CYCLONE
Maxine Hunkel. Teenaged wind witch.
MA HUNKEL
Curator of the JSA brownstone.